TOURISM
PLANNING AND
DEVELOPMENT

TOURISM
PLANNING AND
DEVELOPMENT

Charles Kaiser, Jr., C.P.A.
Larry E. Helber

CBI Publishing Company, Inc.
51 Sleeper Street, Boston, Massachusetts 02210

Library of Congress Cataloging in Publication Data
Kaiser, Charles, 1934-
    Tourism planning and development.

    Includes index.
    1. Tourist trade. 2. Resorts. I. Helber, Larry E., 1937-
    joint author. II. Title.
B155.A1K26   338.4'7'91   77-14474
ISBN   0-8436-2128-1

Printed in the United States

CBI Publishing Company, Inc.
51 Sleeper Street
Boston, Massachusetts 02210

CONTENTS

FOREWORD

In its opening chapter this book points out that in 1975 (the last year for which definitive statistics are currently available) the World Tourism Organization reported some 213 million international travel arrivals. The authors of this book then predict that international tourism is currently "on a plateau waiting to climb dramatically again." Certainly, our experience in the hectic summer of 1977 bears out these prospects.

Although such figures are important indicators of global prospects for economic exchange and growth, we at First Travel Corporation, because of our orientation, are inclined to interpret the numbers from a singular standpoint. We see international travel in 1975 as having involved 213 million personal experiences, each a challenge and opportunity in its own right. We also see this volume as involving billions of transactions between hundreds of thousands of professionals.

Herein lies the real value of this book. Both the scale and rate of growth experienced in recent years by tourism have tended to increase the fragmentation which is the reality of the travel marketplace. Though it is commonly referred to as an industry, tourism is more properly a cluster of separate enterprises attempting to pull itself together around the common interest of its multibillion-dollar proportions. Tourism professionals speak many languages and follow many disciplines. These individuals practice a wide variety of specialties related only through the continuity of the pleasant experience for travelers which is, necessarily, their common goal.

It is in recognizing and making clear this continuity of the tourist's experience that this book imparts a valuable perspective for a wide range of readers. For decision makers involved in any facet of tourism, the methodology in this book provides a practical handle for taking hold of the innumerable details necessary for effective planning and development. Within this framework, each decision maker knows where he or she fits and how this position interrelates with that of other essential contributors to overall success.

Each organization or individual involved in or about to enter the tourism field can profitably look to the content of this book as a model upon which both separate and collective success can be built. For me, the reading of this manuscript has established a valuable set of guidelines which will be put to good and frequent use in evaluating the soundness of planning and development for areas or destinations — and for weighing the likelihood that travelers will enjoy and/or benefit from their visits. If enough people, in enough corners of the world and segments of tourism endeavors, accept and adhere to the principles presented here, we may, in fact, be able to look forward to the day when tourism can be regarded as a coherent industry.

I certainly am glad this work is becoming available and hold high hopes for the continuing extension of professionalism which it should facilitate. My congratulations to Chuck Kaiser for his in-depth thinking and, more significantly still, for reducing these thoughts to writing so that the pages which follow give the reader a comprehensive view of our complex industry.

Van Nuys, California
August 15, 1977

Peter V. Ueberroth
Chairman
First Travel Corporation

PREFACE

In today's economic and political environment, one industry, more truly a segment of the economy, moves to the forefront as the greatest single opportunity for economic, cultural, and political exchange. Tourism, in its broadest, generic sense, can do more to develop understanding among people, provide jobs, create foreign exchange, and raise living standards than any other economic force known.

In direct contrast with the petroleum industry based on fossil fuels, tourism is not dependent on a diminishing resource. To the contrary, tourism, to flourish, must upgrade the environment and maintain the ecological balance. Crime and poverty are deterents to tourism, as are polluted waterways, unkempt beaches, and otherwise despoiled natural and man-made attractions.

Recognizing such potential through numerous studies conducted by the authors and their associates since the conclusion of hostilities following World War II, we believe that the planning and development of tourism are now so sophisticated as to require proper documentation, leading to the writing of this book, which we hope will serve as a model for future projects. There is unlimited potential for tourism development. If improperly conceived and executed, however, such development will prove not only to be financially disastrous, but will also inhibit full realization of improved understanding among diverse people throughout the world — one of the intangible but vital byproducts of tourism growth.

It is our sincere hope that this book will make a substantial contribution to the building of the intellectual preparedness and operational skills essential for continuing international development of tourism. With this need in mind, the book has been aimed at a broad prospective audience which includes undergraduate college students; graduate students; tourism planning and management officials; public and private-sector administrators; hotel and resort executive and management personnel; airline executives and other travel-industry personnel; tourism marketing professionals, including travel agents, media representatives, and employees of tourism agencies; persons involved in national, regional, and international travel associations; researchers, statisticians, accountants, and consultants involved in tourism development; architects and land planners; bankers and other investors, and, far from least, educators building curricula for entry-level employees of tourism entities.

The ensuing book, by its nature, covers multiple disciplines and, therefore, represents a cooperative effort of many people. Although it would be impossible to acknowledge everyone who either made a direct contribution to this volume or who influenced the thinking of the authors, there are certain people whose contributions have been so profound that some recognition is necessary. With respect to economics, the authors are indebted to Dr. John Summerfield of Los Angeles, for his contribution. In the disciplines of architecture and planning, the authors also acknowledge the advice and guidance of George J. (Pete) Wimberly of Honolulu, Hawaii, with whom they have worked on numerous projects.

Particular thanks must be given to Robert A. Peattie, Jr., National Director of Marketing Services of Harris, Kerr, Forster & Company, for his invaluable contributions on transportation and marketing. Also, the authors acknowledge the contributions of James R. Bell and Edward L. Inskeep of Belt, Collins and Associates, Ltd., for their inputs, primarily in the planning areas.

From a coordinating and contributing perspective, this text could not have been developed without the assistance of Bruce Baltin, who directs the Management Advisory Services staff in the Los Angeles office of Harris, Kerr, Forster & Company. Assisting Mr. Baltin in this project were Patrick Quek and Suzanne Hamilton, who also are based in the Los Angeles office of Harris, Kerr, Forster & Company. Additional input and editorial assistance were provided by George E. Lipp, Partner, in the Honolulu office of Harris, Kerr, Forster & Company.

Among the people who had great influence on the authors and for whom the authors have had the pleasure of conducting tourism studies are Alexandre M. Ata, Director General of the Tahiti Tourist Development Board; Alan Greenway, former Chairman, and Basil Atkinson, former General Manager, of the Australian Tourist Commission, and Miss A. Mehta, Joint Director General of India's Department of Tourism. Our thanks also to Marvin Plake, immediate past Executive Vice President, and Stanton Reed, Director of Marketing, for the Pacific Area Travel Association (PATA), whose contributions to tourism development in the Pacific have served as a model of what can be done in this industry.

Of course, my sincere appreciation to my coauthor, Larry E. Helber, who took up the pen after the untimely passing of Walter Collins, with whom I started on this project several years ago. It is, of course, to Walter Collins' memory that this book is dedicated.

And finally, my thanks to all my Partners at Harris, Kerr, Forster & Company who supported my efforts and committed the resources for the writing and publication of this book. To all of them and to the many mentioned and unmentioned, I express my gratitude.

Los Angeles, California
July 25, 1977

Charles Kaiser, Jr., C.P.A.
Managing Partner
Harris, Kerr, Forster & Company

1

PLANNING: THE KEY TO SUCCESS

PEOPLE ARE TOURISTS

Since before — and throughout — recorded time, the horizon has always been irresistible. People have to see what is on the other side. People travel. People visit. People have a seemingly insatiable curiosity about someplace else.

As people have grouped together and formed societies, some individuals have always had a bursting need to get away. Sometimes the need was for elbow room, or living room. As societies grew, a natural human tendency to seek more space and better living conditions took the form of colonization. Then as economic prosperity spread, the need for a temporary change of scenery, environment, or experience or a rediscovery of heritage became even greater driving forces, leading to tourism on an organized, large-scale basis.

With industrialization and the routines of work and lifestyle imposed upon wage earners and their families, society institutionalized — and continually lengthened — the annual vacation. As mobility increased through trains, cars, and ultimately airplanes, people popularized the mini-vacation built around long weekends. Faster, longer-range travel has assumed a cause-effect relationship with the basic human desire to look at someplace else. The further, faster, and less expensively people have been able to wander, the more extensively they have traveled. Today, one-week or two-week tour packages transcend distances which used to encompass lifetimes of travel.

ECONOMICS AND DISTANCE

Man's propensity to travel is axiomatic. This is proven by the extent to which vacation-travel horizons have been extended. As an illustration, consider the situation of Hawaii. Prior to World War II, Waikiki, was a sparsely developed luxury spot. It served as a playground for the comparatively few people who could afford leisurely cruises to the islands at relatively high costs.

As quickly as airline routes were opened and fares and facilities came within the reach of masses of poeple in such markets as the U.S. mainland and Japan, demand rose to meet the available capacities. Costs of and time for travel decreased with the advent of jets, then wide-bodied aircraft, stimulating demand further.

Hawaii's example, which applies equally to many other locations all over the world, serves to prove that human beings have a basic, innate desire to travel. They will visit any attractive place within their means and the timing constraints of the social structure which exists during any given period.

This mounting urge of people to travel is easily demonstrated: in 1960, international tourism arrivals as reported by the World Tourism Organization, totaled approximately 71 million. In 1975, the figure was 213 million. At this writing, indications are that tourism is on a plateau waiting to climb dramatically again.

The importance of the change of pace offered by vacations is evidenced further by the emphasis placed on the length of vacation, the number of holidays, and other leisure-time considerations in labor-management bargaining in recent years. On the other side, increasing numbers of employers have emphasized vacation benefits in their recruiting. Governmental agencies, for example, regularly feature vacation benefits as offsetting the higher wages available in industry in many areas. In recruiting personnel for jobs in remote or undesirable areas, such as Alaska's North Slope, frequent and extensive vacation travel paid for by employers has been a major factor, over and above wage scales dictated by supply-and-demand conditions.

In summary, tourism attractions which represent a change in lifestyle and routine for large numbers of people appear to meet a basic and continually expanding demand.

WHAT IS TOURISM?

The point has been made that tourism is largely inevitable. But just what is the inevitability? In this book, the term, *tourism* is applied to discretionary travel by individuals and families. Although the World Tourism Organization (an agency of the United Nations) includes all travelers in their definition of tourism, the authors have excluded business personnel whose travel requirements are mandated. The book is concerned with the discretionary traveler susceptible to marketing programs which can enhance tourism volumes. Accordingly, the subject matter encompasses all aspects of discretionary travel, as well as the related activities and associated or sustaining services.

Discretionary travel, by nature of that term, excludes travel specifically for business, military, educational, therapeutic, or family visitation purposes. However, tourism can encompass activities or travel related to such stimuli. For example, the businessman attending a convention or trade show frequently stays in an area for several days after the conclusion of his business and becomes a tourist.

In using the term, tourism, inclusively, the authors intend to encompass all of the activities and impacts associated with discretionary travel, international and domestic. Various aspects of tourism and associated services are covered in separate, individual chapters of this book. For the purposes of the present discussion, however, it is important to recognize that, if tourism is regarded inclusively, the planning and management processes associated with tourism must be integrated to encompass the whole scope of discretionary travel, as well as sufficiently inclusive and comprehensive to deal with ever-increasing breadth.

SCOPE OF TOURISM

Economically, tourism holds a unique position. It is not properly an industry. Rather it takes in a cross section of the entire economy for a region or nation. The impact of tourism revenues and activities cuts across many skill areas, industries, and segments of a population. In many geographic areas, a major value for tourism development lies in the fact that it employs and offers career opportunities for comparatively large numbers of unskilled, entry-level workers.

For these and many other reasons, tourism is unquestionably a major factor in the economies of many nations and in international trade.

Tourism also exists and functions on a far less grandiose scale. Individual resorts, hotels, or visitor attractions are a basic, critical part of the tourism picture. Individual attractions or facilities can either stimulate or respond to regional or national tourism programs. For planning and management purposes, the challenges are pretty much similar for an individual attraction or property as they are for an area or nation, though there will be vast differences in scope and scale.

MEETING THE DEMANDS

Combining the natural desire of people to travel with their increasing affluence, it follows that money, in substantial amounts, is spent on tourism. It is basic to human nature that when such a condition exists, suppliers will materialize to accommodate the spenders. Tourism accommodation, locally and on an international basis, has become a big busines. In the state of California alone, revenues for tourism and associated activities are estimated at $5 billion annually. For the United States, tourism revenue for 1974, as published by the U.S. Travel Data Center, was $60 billion. According to the World Tourism Organization, international tourism revenues amounted to some $319 billion in 1975.

These figures, as impressive as they may be, tell only a part of the story. Since tourism is really a collection of industries, enterprises, resources, and attractions, it is impossible for anything so diverse to be recorded in cohesive, unified statistics. For example, take the ordinary international vacation trip. Travelers use airlines, local bus transportation, subways, hotels, restaurants, retail establishments, theaters, motion picture houses, sports facilities, and many other resources of the host area. It would be virtually impossible to establish a financial-reporting system which brought all of these data together.

Thus, although tourism has assumed major economic proportions, an industry, in the literal sense of this term, has never materialized. Rather, fragmentation has been the rule. Individuals or groups have built hotels, restaurants, attractions, or capitalized in one way or another on resources such as beaches, mountains, lakes, rivers, cities, customs, or cultures.

THE BOOM-BUST CYCLE

This has been true for entities or management groups in both the private and public sectors of the areas involved. Governmental agencies have been just as shortsighted and as lax in their planning as profit-motivated capitalists. Where planning and commitment have been lacking, greed and other base human tendencies have taken control by default. When this has happened, tourist attractions or resorts have tended to pattern themselves into rising-and-falling, feast-or-famine cycles. Almost anybody who has followed tourism can describe a resort which started as a playground for the wealthy, became increasingly popular, experienced a cycle of feverish building and capital investment, hit a heyday, then began to decline.

A catechism of horrors is not necessary to illustrate this point. A single example dramatizes what can happen in a relatively short time and in a seemingly uncontrollable fashion. Consider Atlantic City, New Jersey. The basic resources here were an excellent beach, a relatively temperate summer climate, and splendid surf. To this, early developers added amenities which quickly became famous, attractive, and known worldwide through Parker Brothers' popular game, *Monopoly*. Local government agencies built an amusement pier and boardwalk. Private interests added luxury hotels. During the 1920s and into the 1930s, Atlantic City thrived as a luxury resort.

Then a convention center was added to put things on a big scale. Additional hotel and motel facilities were constructed on every available lot in proximity to the ocean. Atlantic City didn't have the population to serve and support these seasonal facilities. Help had to be recruited from cities of the Northeast. To accommodate employees and other non-luxury tenants, rooming-house colonies began to crowd the luxury facilities. These dwellings were dreary in appearance and minimal in investment. Before long, they deteriorated into urban blight, crowding the hotels and depressing the environs. In the face of changing travel patterns, particularly the air age, the fate of Atlantic City was almost predictable.

The presence of the convention center and the mobs it attracted served as a disinclination for the clientele of the former luxury hotels. These establishments, in their turn, began to deteriorate.

The lesson here is that planners should look behind and beyond the intitial prosperity which tourism development promises. Overutilization or inadequate planning can open the door for potential disaster.

(In November, 1976, New Jersey voters passed a referendum legalizing gaming in Atlantic City. This action may revitalize the city's tourism activity. However, this change in the attraction basis of the area will, in itself, require extensive new planning to derive potential benefits while avoiding possible drawbacks.)

UPS AND DOWNS IN TOURIST BEHAVIOR

A psychological theory has been advanced to explain the apparently patterned rise and fall in popularity of tourism destination areas. The authors first encountered this theory in a presentation in the fall of 1972 by its developer, Stanley C. Plog, president of Behavior Science Corporation.

Mr. Plog places the behavior characteristics of travelers in a continuum of "psychographic" groups. Two major behavior polarities are identified:

- Allocentric persons are self-confident, usually successful, high earners, and frequent travelers. Allocentrics tend to prefer uncrowded destinations where they can satisfy a desire for discovery through novel experiences. They show a high interest in meeting people and exploring strange cultures.

- Psychocentric persons are unsure of themselves, employed in mundane positions, low earners, and infrequent travelers who seek the security of tours to familiar destinations.

Between these extremes are gradations: near-allocentric, mid-centric, and near-psychocentric. The great majority of people are judged by Mr. Plog to be mid-centric. Mid-centric tastes run to budget tours, heavily used destination points, familiar food, and chain-type hotels.

Tourism destinations, Mr. Plog holds, tend to rise and fall in cycles which match shifting psychographic appeal. Mr. Plog described the phenomenon this way:

> They (resorts) move through the continuum, on a consistent basis, from appealing first to allocentrics and last to psychocentrics. The first people to "discover" a new area are the allocentrics. They enjoy the sense of discovery and like to immerse themselves in new activities while there is still a sense of naturalness about them. As allocentrics begin talking to their friends about recent vacations, these travel destinations can become the "in spots." This leads to a larger market for these resort areas and they are now being visited by a near-allocentric group of travelers. The near-allocentrics are not the discoverers, but they are close behind and the increased number of travelers they represent leads to the development of hotels, restaurants, and the usual tourist facilities in the specific resort area. Thus, we can see that the resort destination is beginning to move along a continuum on our psychographic scale in terms of the type of traveler it attracts.
>
> As a destination becomes more popular, the mid-centric audience begins to pick it up. The continued increase of travelers leads to further development of the resort, in terms of hotels, tourist shops, scheduled activities for tourists, and the usual services that are provided in a "mature" resort area. By this time, the allocentrics are turned off by the destination because it has lost its sense of naturalness and a smaller number of near-allocentrics are also visiting.
>
> The destination has reached its maximum potential because it is now attracting the broadest audience possible. Until now, the introduction of each new type of traveler has meant a larger population base from which to draw travelers. There are more near-allocentrics than allocentrics and many more mid-centrics than near-allocentrics. However, continued tourist development of the area carries with it the threat of the destruction of the area as a viable tourist resort. When the appeal of the resort passes the magic midpoint in the population curve of travelers, several critical things happen. The destination is now appealing to an audience which is composed mostly of mid-centrics to near-psychocentrics. From this point on, as the destination moves toward the psychocentric end of the continuum in terms of its appeal in popularity, it begins to draw on a smaller number of travelers. (It is approaching a declining curve.) More important, however, these travelers have characteristics about them which make them a difficult audience to attract. Though the destination may appeal to them because it has become very popular and, by its *popularity,* convinces them that it is a worthwhile resort area, psychocentrics do not travel as often as allocentrics and they prefer those destinations that they can get to and from their homes easily by automobile. Further, their total stay at the destination is

less than for allocentrics, and they spend less on a per capita daily basis.

Thus, we can visualize a destination moving across the spectrum, however gradually or slowly, but far too often inexorably toward the potential of its own demise. Destination areas carry with them the potential seeds of their own destruction, as they allow themselves to become more commercialized and lose their qualities which originally attracted tourists.

The psychographic continuum and its relationship to the market positions of some well-known tourism destinations is shown in Figure 1-1.

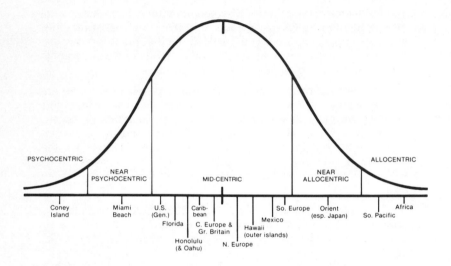

FIGURE 1-1

IS DECLINE INEVITABLE?

Does this psychogenic pattern impact all tourism destinations?

Is there an inevitable failure ahead for every tourism success?

The evidence can certainly be frightening. Hopefully, the prospects of an extreme psychocentric fate will lead increasing numbers of tourism decision makers to pause for some serious thought about the market identity of their destination points — and about the future image they wish to see develop. Such a pause, its associated thought processes, and the documentation of resulting decisions and commitments form the heart of tourism planning.

When such planning takes place, evidence shows, decline can be avoided. More to the point: success can be predicted, achieved, and sustained.

The most apparent common denominators which can be identified with destinations in decline from a high rate of apparent success is a lack of planning toward and maintenance of an established market identity. Each of these destinations permitted its image — and the use of its resources — to veer away from the strengths upon which its success was built.

On the positive side, many strong, continuing success stories within the tourism field describe destinations which have undergone thorough planning, supported by solid commitments for their attainment. Some examples:

- New Orleans established and built a substantial tourism industry based on the charm of its French Quarter. Uncompromising care has been taken to protect and expand upon this appeal. New attractions and facilities have conformed to the established decor — or they have been developed in locations accessible to but outside of this tourist hub. These additional attractions and facilties have included a major convention center, the Louisiana Superdome, and several high-rise hotels.

- Victoria, British Columbia, and Mackinac Island, Michigan, have succeeded with old-fashioned images. Both have historic, Victorian-era features protected and publicized through policies which prohibit the use of automobiles in the respective resort areas, as does Bermuda.

- Williamsburg, Virginia, has built solid success through the quality with which it has carried out restoration to its historic Colonial state and maintained its charm.

- Disneyland, in California, and Disney World, in Florida, have maintained success through careful monitoring of the quality of services and the protection of the family image to which these theme parks and their accompanying hotels were built. For example, beer and liquor are never served in these parks even though substantial initial revenue increases could result from a change in policy.

There are, fortunately, many other success stories. All share the common denominators of sound, thorough planning followed by meticulous implementation of plans and careful maintenance of image and market position.

These comparisons between management practices marked by boom-and-decline cycles and those where success has been sustained lead to conclusions that:

1. Strong attractions for identified segments of a tourism market are essential to success.

2. Given the presence of suitable attractions, planning, commitment, and management are prime elements in determining the difference between ultimate decline or sustained success.

Beyond these, there are, unfortunately, no universal rules which assure success if followed. Each area, each attraction, each section of a city, each resort or hotel property has its own potential for accommodation, its own saturation point, and its own economic infrastructure. The break-even point for tourism as an industry will vary with areas and attractions. Initially, there will be a break-even point which calls for attracting a certain number of tourists with a certain amount of discretionary income. Beyond that, the ratios begin to change.

MANAGING RESOURCES

The key, obviously, lies in managing available resources responsibly. But who is responsible? Where does the buck stop? Where is the power nominally? Where is it really?

There are no pat answers. There are, however, some basic truths. Predominant among these are that singleness of purpose equates to success; devisiveness builds downfall. This is true whether the decision powers are held by the private or public sector within the area.

Too often, members of the public sector or the private sector blame each other for an area's problems. This is an example of devisiveness. Private-sector investors let their properties run down because they are convinced that responsible government bodies will not do what it takes to maintain an area or to help it continue to grow. Conversely, frightened public officials can and have constrained the economy and facilities of an area to a point where accommodations capabilities have become strangulated.

Public and Private Sectors

Even the very terms public sector and private sector can be misnomers where tourism is concerned. Normally, the public sector takes in all governmental agencies or responsibilities. Typically, this would include airports, roads, facilities, beaches, forest lands, and all zoning and land utilization policies and decisions. Consider a situation, however, where a developer or a group of developers becomes large enough so that its employees and supporters represent the majority of the votes in an area.

Where a corporation has created a "company-town" environment, has it not become, in a *de facto* sense, an embodiment of the public sector? Does it not have the same responsibilities, whether or not they are recognized and/or assumed? The point is that the power for decisions and for actions, in such a situation, rests with a single, managed group. One or a few decision-level managers can make commitments which impact the future of their area and its inhabitants.

In such situations, the key to tourism success or failure lies in recognizing the existence of the power to make things happen and the need for controlled, concerted, planned action. Where this power is recognized and exercised with due care, tourism will flourish and enjoy a continuity of prosperity. The real danger lies in lack of recognition. This can result in short sightedness or mismanagement of resources.

The converse situation occurs when there is devisiveness. A typical cause for divided interest in management occurs when a change of management has taken place, either in the public or the private sector. For example, a local or municipal administration may encourage the development of tourism. Private interests may invest capital and begin to develop facilities. An election ensues. A new administration changes policy and tries to put things back the way they were. At this point, reinstatement of the former status quo is a serious change. In the conflict which evolves, the area and its inhabitants are bound to be losers.

A particularly dramatic example of a political change which impacted a major tourism industry can be seen in Cuba. Prior to 1958, Cuba was the leading destination point for Caribbean tourism. Almost overnight, tourist facilities were virtually closed down.

A lesser, but still dramatic, impact was seen in the massive cancellation suffered by tourism accommodations in Mexico following a vote by that country's representative to the United Nations in favor of a resolution equating Zionism with racism. Tourism dropped sharply and immediately. It takes considerable effort and fence mending to overcome the impact upon tourism of a political decision made with other considerations in mind, if, indeed, the effect can ever be overcome fully.

Nationalism has also had a recent, adverse impact upon other Caribbean nations. Wanton shooting of tourists at luxury golf resorts does little to enhance the appeal of a destination. Neither do crime and poverty attract visitors.

In summary, in adopting tourism-related platforms, policies, and committed plans, a long-range outlook is essential, since tourism development requires equillibrium. If this equillibrium is interrupted or altered, the future potential of an area may be destroyed at worst, set back substantially at best.

FACTS OF TOURISM LIFE

Recognition of responsibility and responsible action, then, become the essential, initial ingredients for either coping with or deriving benefits from tourism. Note the choice between coping and benefitting. This is really the major choice open to planning and management. Given the presence of attractions and some hospitality, tourism will occur. People will travel. In traveling, in today's society, they will spend money. If they spend money, they will be accommodated. In the course of providing accommodation, the resources of an area, both natural and created, will be utilized.

Control of resources, then, carries with it a large measure of responsibility. In some few instances, the environment and resources of sizable areas are responsive to decisions of individuals or companies — the private sector. In most cases, however, the reasoning prevails that the environment and its resources belong to the people who inhabit an area. Given this outlook, responsibility and accountability for tourism management lie with the government empowered to represent those people.

Where both public and private-sector entities play roles in an area's tourism, there is a good probability that they will, at some point, find themselves at cross purposes. Theoretically, this should not be so. A reasoning outlook will hold that if an area prospers in its entirety, all of its parts or elements will also prosper. Thus, if a company owned a hotel at a seashore, as long as people are attracted to that resort and are willing to pay a reasonable price for rooms and services, everyone should prosper — hotel owners, people seeking employment, support industries in the area, and even uninvolved taxpayers who derive benefits from the substantial tax base created.

But things do not always work out that way. If an area, for example shows any strong signs of downturn, hotel management may well decide to reduce investments in maintenance and reconstruction in favor of higher immediate profits and payout. The property declines and so do rates which can be charged. This, in turn, contributes to the overall decline of the area. The hotel manager may blame the local legislature. The local citizens may blame the hotel for inadequate maintenance of the property.

When devisiveness occurs, everybody loses. Unity of purpose, plan, and action, on the other hand, will be common denominators for sustained success. These are the real, basic facts of tourism life. Successful tourism development is literally, dependent upon effective planning. The initial challenge lies in orienting plans toward success. This, in turn, is the subject for the next chapter.

SYNOPSIS

Travel and exploration are basic to human nature. These traits underlie growth of tourism to a 1975 international volume of $319 billion, according to the World Tourism Organization.

In tourism, success is neither guaranteed nor permanent. To the contrary, many areas have experienced tourism cycles which start with few, affluent visitors, proceed through a series of expansion programs, attain saturation, then go into a decline. If an eventual decline is to be avoided, responsible planning and management are essential.

A recognition of this need for planning and management responsibility and authority is an essential which is prerequisite to tourism success. In most situations, this authority and its accompanying responsibility are in the province of and must be assumed by governmental (public sector) entities. This establishing of authority and responsibility for tourism planning and management is an essential, initial step toward tourism success.

REVIEW QUESTIONS

1. What is tourism? Define and describe.

2. Describe the boom-and-decline (psychographic continuum) which has afflicted many tourism areas.

3. Explain the importance and value of careful, long-range planning for tourism development.

4. Describe the roles of the public and private sectors in the tourism industry of your area, or of another area with which you may be familiar.

5. Based upon knowledge or experience about your own area or another area with which you may be familiar, think about and describe steps which could help avoid an eventual tourism decline.

2

PLANNING AND SUCCESS

THE STAGES OF SUCCESS

Tourists come to an area or a resort for enjoyment. They seek a pleasant experience. Hopefully, success in tourism will result in a pleasant, successful experience for the destination as well. This is the real planning and management challenge.

Actually, success for a tourism destination breaks down into two logical stages, or phases:

1. Building success

2. Maintaining success.

BUILDING SUCCESS

For a tourism destination, success almost invariably tends to be measured in terms of growth. This applies whether the destination is an individual resort facility within a highly developed region, an area of an emerging nation, or encom-

15

passes an entire country. The objective is the same: tourism represents growth.

Consider: the tourist comes to a destination and spends money without demanding any tangible assets or product in return. In other words, tourism adds to the wealth of the destination. This contribution can be substantial.

In calculating the impact of tourism, a multiplier factor is frequently considered. This is discussed more fully in a later chapter. But for overview purposes, it is valuable to understand that expenditures by tourists are recycled through the economy in the form of investments, wages, taxes, purchases of goods and services, consumables, and so on. Economists use varying multiplier factors to estimate the impact of tourism. The actual impact will vary widely between areas, depending on the local economy and the extent to which it is otherwise self-sustaining. In general, the higher the dependence upon tourism and imports, the lower the multiplier factor will be. This is because an area which depends heavily on tourism will probably have to import many of the goods and services the tourists and its own people need. Conversely, areas with highly diversified economies will have higher multiplier factors because the funds are recycled through the economy more than they are in relatively undeveloped areas.

Even in an area with a relatively low multiplier, tourism can have a substantial impact. Consider, for example, a rural area in a country which is considered to be an emerging nation. Suppose the average income of the population at the time a tourism attraction is opened is in the range of $1,000 per family, per year. A family of four visiting a resort in this area for a two-week vacation might spend, let us say, $2,000. Allowing that this is recycled through the economy 2.5 times, the economic impact of this one visit is equivalent to the previous total annual income for five families in the area. If an attraction is planned so that tourism visits run into the tens of thousands or hundreds of thousands annually, the impact could be extensive. Without planning, it could actually be shocking. For the purpose of this discussion, however, let us consider this type of potential income as an opportunity rather than concentrating on its potential problems.

Let us assume also that a destination has or can secure the know-how, the financing, the operational and technical support, and the marketing necessary to capitalize upon its tourism potential. Let us assume further that managers in the public sector, the governmental agencies in this area, are aware of the potential pitfalls and are committed to realizing balanced, constructive, creative growth through planned development of their tourism potential. They realize that there is more to tourism success than simply opening their customs and immigration doors and waiting for the revenue to flow. They realize that tourists come to seek an environment of natural and man-made beauty, that they expect to meet friendly, well-trained personnel, to encounter and learn about other cultures, and to do all this in a pleasant, friendly atmosphere.

In other words, it is assumed that the public-sector managers in this hypothetic destination are aware that tourism, reduced to basics, is an experience in sharing. These, admittedly, are major assumptions. For now, however, let us assume enlightenment and good intent.

Given the existence of these factors, success in the building of a tourism destination can be seen as centering around a formula of four E's:

- Economics
- Environment
- Enrichment (social and financial)
- Exchange.

Economics

The economics of tourism success for any given destination lie in determining optimum levels of activity for bringing in the greatest feasible amount of revenue provided that:

1. Levels of tourism activity are such that new tourists and returnees will be pleased and will continue to visit the area

2. The economy of the area itself can absorb and make good use of these revenues

3. The resources of the area are not despoiled or unnecessarily depleted.

Intakes of funds which are either too little to do enough good for the sacrifices involved or are too great to be absorbed constructively could have a destructive effect. Thus, a prime challenge in planning for success lies in setting goals which identify and spell out what the economic impact of tourism should be.

Environment

In most cases, environment *is* tourism. People come to an attraction or destination because of its climate, its scenic beauty, or its man-made attractions. People also travel to be with other people. Thus, in a broad sense, people and customs are very much an integral part of a tourism environment. Under this interpretation, a tourism impact which despoils customs, religion, dress, or lifestyle, would have just as destructive an effect as littering, trampling the grass, or overcrowding which destroyed beaches or forests.

All too often, tourism debases the very resources which brought the tourists in the first place. Using the environment without using it up, therefore, is one of the key challenges and prerequisites for tourism success.

In considering environment as a building block for tourism, it is essential that planners take a comprehensive look at all of their environmental assets. Environment is a totality rather than a collection of individual parts. Thus, beaches, surf, climate, green belts, friendly people, historic monuments, the relationship of buildings to their surroundings, historic landmarks, traffic and pedestrian circulation, and many other facets are all part of a total. Sacrificing any part for short-range tourism gain can lead to the long-range degradation of attraction for tourists, thus initiating a self-defeating cycle. An objective of tourism planning, then, is enhancement of attractiveness which brings people to the area in the first place.

This is not to say that modernization and new buildings always go hand-in-hand with tourism development. The experience of Colonial Williamsburg, in Virginia, has proved that just the opposite can be true. This renowned tourism destination actually built success by turning back the calendar architecturally. In 1930, Colonial Williamsburg started a massive program with an initial donation from the Rockefeller Foundation for the restoration of a substantial portion of the town to the conditions which prevailed prior to the American Revolution. This proved an attraction which has drawn many millions of visitors. It also started a trend which has seen restored villages and towns emerge as a major category of tourism attractions around the world.

Planners should keep in mind that the natural, or physical, environment and the people who inhabit it are closely related. Plans and programs must enhance the physical environment for its indigenous residents as well as for the tourists who will visit. Tourism achieved only at a sacrifice for the inhabitants of an area will ultimately suffer adverse social and economic consequences. Everyone has to win. Any note of hostility in the attitudes or actions of residents toward tourists will be quickly felt at the collective cash register for the destination. The Caribbean is probably as good an example as can be found of a situation where environment was exploited for the sake of tourism on one island after another. Inevitably, reactions of indigenous populations set in. These reactions, in turn, led to serious declines in tourism activity.

Enrichment

The need for enrichment relates closely to the considerations associated with environment. The lives and lifestyles, even the cultural heritages of persons in the destination area, should be enriched if a tourism plan is to succeed. Enrichment, it should be stressed, does not automatically equate to refrigerators and washing machines. Prosperity is expected. But it need not obliterate the culture or customs of the area into which it is introduced.

(As an illustration, consider the ultra modern, highly respected Museum of Archeology in Mexico City. This is a world-renowned institution made possible in some measure by Mexico's tourism success. It builds an appreciation of the heritage of Mexico for the country's own people and for all the world. This is just one example. Other countries have demonstrated similarly their ability to keep their culture and heritage intact in the face of industrialization, modernization, and tourism success.)

For developing countries, the fact that tourism and enrichment of a host-area population go hand-in-hand is demonstrated by the growth of academic activity and the building of universities which have traditionally accompanied tourism success. Typically, local residents begin attending secondary schools and universities in the country of origin of the majority of its tourists. Ultimately, these people return to contribute to the development of universities in their own countries. The cultural interchange implicit in this type of development contributes, in turn, to international understanding and a mutuality of growth.

Planners should keep in mind also that tourists themselves frequently have enrichment as one of their own objectives for traveling to an area. They wish to learn about and enrich their own experience through contact with the people and the customs of the countries they visit.

Exchange

The element of exchange involves all of the foregoing items. Economic exchange should favor the tourism destination. Opportunities for economic development should, if planning is sufficiently broad, extend beyond the immediate income of tourist expenditures. Many tourists are successful persons who can influence future relationships between their own companies or countries and areas they visit. A vacation frequently marks an introductory experience which leads to investment or trade opportunities. The better the tourism planners prepare for such contingencies, the more likely they are to happen.

Part of this economic planning must be a recognition that all involved parties must gain. If a country hopes to attract capital, it must be prepared to provide an attractive return for investors. International investment is a volatile field. A region or country wishing to attract foreign capital must be prepared to commit to and work for the success of investors, as well as for their own region or nation. This, unfortunately, is a lesson which has not always been learned in time.

This is also an area where naivete can be disastrous. There is a danger, for example, that an area which has known poverty in the past will find its people becoming overly materialistic. Similarly, there is a danger that an area which attracts tourists because it represents a good economic value will experience inflation which, in time, drives the tourists away.

The same is true of attitudes. it is not uncommon that early tourists who visit an area are welcomed warmly and openly, only to find hospitality diminishing in proportion to the prosperity enjoyed. This, in itself, can be the beginning of a decline.

Thus, in planning for and managing a tourism program, it becomes essential to keep in mind and to monitor the exchange factors which contribute to success. Any upsetting of the balance can begin to contribute to a decline.

MAINTAINING SUCCESS

Tourism, by its nature, is dynamic. Tourism means change. The very nature of the business of tourism or of tourists coming to any destination can change dynamically over relatively short periods, as described in Chapter 1. This trend is worth noting here because of the importance of planning in minimizing its impact. The consequences to be avoided through planning are easily illustrated:

Consider the evolution of such destination areas as Miami Beach, Hawaii, and the Costa del Sol area of Spain. Miami Beach has had the longest history. During the 1920s, it attracted relatively few, comparatively wealthy, rail travelers. Middle-income tourists moved in gradually, first by rail coach, then by air. The fact that the area also developed appeal for the "singles" market can be seen in the famous spring invasions of Fort Lauderdale by college students. As facilities built up to accommodate the heavy winter and spring influxes, operators began to see a potential for attracting family visitors over the summer. The development of a major portion of Florida as a family tourism destination has climaxed in recent years with the completion and continuing development of Disney World and other attractions in and around Orlando.

In Hawaii, expansion followed a similar pattern, facilitated when air travel replaced ships as the dominant form of transportation. Mass expansion came with the jet. In 1955, there were 110,000 overnight (or longer) visitors; in 1975, this figure was 2,829,000.

Spain provides an interesting example because of the mixture of origin markets which has led to its tourism growth. Tourists to Spain come largely from the colder European countries. With the opening of trade and travel routes to the U.S., increasing numbers of Americans have also vacationed in Spain.

Such trends can reflect different facets of prosperity. However, it takes a concerted management effort to maintain prosperity and quality without permitting panic or alterations in attitudes and activities which contribute to decline. In short, management of a host area must recognize who its tourists are, what they expect, and what terms of exchange apply. As the mix and makeup of tourism change, the decision makers of a destination must plan for and implement adjusting changes. The consequence of not doing so is a high probability of decline.

Success in tourism, then begins with a willingness and an effective program for building followed by responsive activities aimed at maintaining a predetermined, planned level of success.

PLANNING PREREQUISITES FOR SUCCESS

The picture of tourism success painted thus far can be highly attractive — appealing enough to draw billions of dollars of private and public funding into tourism development each year. Because of the financial, human, and environmental stakes involved, it is important to recognize that *success of tourism ventures is not automatic.* There are some dramatic failures which bear witness to this, including many destination resorts which have gone through bankruptcy and physical decay.

To avoid such fates — and to increase the probabilities of success — decision makers and planners associated with tourism development should establish sound guidelines at the outset, before active planning and development are initiated. Whether a project encompasses a single resort or an entire destination area, some individual or small group starts each development program. At this point, only leaders are involved. As is true for leaders in any field, their job is to convert dreams to stated concepts which can be carried forward by others.

Too often, the communication of these concepts is loose, informal, and easily subject to misinterpretation. The people implementing the concepts can misunderstand or be carried away by their own enthusiasm. To avoid such problems — and to avoid the effects of boom-and-decline cycles — the initiators of a project should establish a set of criteria, policies, and guidelines which will orient their ideas toward success.

To build such a framework for success, the initiators can profitably anticipate and answer a series of questions which persons implementing their ideas should answer. These questions could include, but need not be limited to, the following:

1 . Does the idea call for building upon existing tourism or tapping new markets?

2 . What are the scope and scale of the proposed development?

3 . What area or areas are involved?

4 . What is there about these areas that should attract tourists?

5 . How might tourism impact or change the area or areas?

6 . What limits should be set upon tourism impact, growth, or change?

7. Who would be involved in tourism development and what would be expected of them?

8. What time frame is realistic for this project?

If tourism is to succeed for any developing destination, it is necessary for all involved parties to begin working together as soon as possible — and to establish a mutual commitment for success. Early, logical, clearly understood statements of concepts and policies are important prerequisites in orienting a project toward success.

FRUITS OF SUCCESS

Where planning and management are effective, a destination can realize:

1. Substantial economic growth and benefits to the local community

2. Improvements in quality of life, lifestyle, and cultural opportunities for local inhabitants

3. Economic development through recycling and utilization of tourism revenues

4. Potential benefits through interests and subsequent activities of people who initially encounter an area as tourists

5. Preservation and enhancement of environmental resources. (Tourism is a "clean" industry.)

Examples of the possible value of tourism and visitation generally in building the economies of host areas suitable for industrialization are both easy to identify and quite dramatic. In the United States, both California and Florida have built substantial economies by attracting persons who first visited the areas as military travelers or tourists, then returned to settle and build. California has become the most populous state in the United States largely because of the influx of new settlers.

Conversely, some popular tourism areas have chosen to promote visitation aggressively while discouraging new settlers. Oregon and Hawaii are examples of areas that have enjoyed major tourism growth while adopting educational, economic, and promotional programs specifically to discourage new settlers.

A prominent international example of economic results of an initial visit can be seen in the aftereffects from a chance visit to

Russia, following World War I, by a young physician, Dr. Armand Hammer. The doctor returned to the United States to go into business. He went on to become President of Occidental Petroleum. The relationships established during this initial visit to the Soviet Union have blossomed into transactions accounting for many billions of dollars in trade between the Soviet Union and western nations. In time, these relationships have contributed to a trickling and gradually expanding activity of U.S. tourism to Russia. At this writing, a major international trade center, which includes a western-style hotel, is under development in Moscow. This could lead to additional increases in tourism flow and tourism revenues between the United States and the Soviet Union, provided the international political climate and the relationships between the two governments support such developments.

The spectrum of potential benefit runs through many degrees and gradations. This, in large measure, is the challenge of tourism planning. Decision makers in an area must decide what they want for themselves and their constituents.

SYNOPSIS

A destination derives benefits from tourism development in direct relationship to the efforts expended on planning and management. Given attractions capable of providing a quality enjoyable experience for visitors, it is important to establish criteria, policies, and guidelines at the outset. These should describe what the tourism destination aspires to become — *and* what it does not want to be. In other words, both development goals and constraints should be stated clearly. This should be done in writing and with clear references to anticipated markets, volumes, and areas involved. Such statements should be considered as prerequisites to organized planning and development. If this is done, tourism can be a strong, positive economic force. Inadequate planning, conversely, can increase probabilities of failure or decline.

REVIEW QUESTIONS

1.   Describe the economic benefits which can be realized by a successful tourism destination.

2.   Explain what a preliminary set of tourism-development guidelines should accomplish. Describe briefly the content of such a statement.

3.   Describe steps a tourism destination can take to help maintain its success.

4.   For your area or one with which you are familiar, describe some of the strengths and/or attractions which could contribute to new or further tourism development. Describe these potential contributions and the steps which should be taken.

5.   For your area or one with which you are familiar, describe some real or potential pitfalls in tourism development. Discuss ways in which these might be avoided or their effects minimized.

3

A PROCESS FOR TOURISM PLANNING

THE NECESSITY OF PLANNING

If an area, region, or country possesses attractions and provides some hospitality for prospective travelers, tourism will probably develop. If this tourism is to benefit the host area, formal, forward-looking planning is essential.

Recognition of this situation is widespread enough so that tourism planning and management have become an established, growing professional endeavor. A variety of organizations dedicated to the planning and managing (as distinct from marketing and operating) of tourism programs already exists. A number of universities and colleges offer two-year, four-year, and graduate curricula in tourism, travel, hotel, and restaurant management. In addition, a nucleus of consulting organizations has emerged specifically in the tourism planning and development area. This was one logical result of worldwide tourism growth. All of the characteristics which have stimulated development of consulting specialties elsewhere have come to exist in the tourism field. For example:

- Development of a major tourism facility, attraction, or destination is a major undertaking using considerable amounts of money, natural resources, technical expertise, political and cultural resources, and human effort.

- The technological natures of area, land, architectural, landscaping, environmental impact, sewage, water, financial management, and other disciplines necessary to tourism development lend themselves naturally to the application of consulting-type expertise.

- Because planning and development programs are of a one-time, project nature, they do not lend themselves to permanent employment of all required personnel. Consulting organizations specialize in such engagements.

- Almost inevitably, financial and other assistance or support will be needed from sources outside the destination area. These external partners invariably insist upon objective appraisals and evaluations of the prospects for tourism plans and programs. This objectivity requirement cannot usually be satisfied by employees of sponsoring tourism agencies.

- Finally, project management has become an area of expertise unto itself. This expertise is propagated and nurtured largely by consulting-type organizations. Experience has proven that tourism development projects lend themselves naturally to application of these skills.

Having arrived at the status of necessity, the art of tourism planning and management has also evolved into a quasi-science which has, in turn, spawned its own technologies and methodologies. These, in essence, are the tools of the tourism planning and management trade whose application is covered in the remainder of this book.

THE SPECIFIC STIMULUS FOR PLANNING

If tourism planning is to happen in a specific area, someone, or some entity must stimulate and enunciate the original idea. This basic inspiration must be shared by the party or entity which holds controlling interest and responsibility for the resources to be utilized by the tourism industry.

This principal holds true for a planning program of any scope or dimension. For example, there may be an existing hotel, resort, or industry in a region. The stimulus may be realization that there is potential for growth if only existing facilities can be expanded or new ones generated. At the other extreme, an area may have potential but undeveloped resources, along with some economic motivation to stimulate tourism and its associated revenues.

No matter what the situation, if tourism planning is to begin, there must be active involvement by persons or entities controlling the essential resources. Other parties — political, financial and technological — will have to be involved. But active participation by the controllers of the essential resources is an irreducible requirement. Depending upon individual situations, forms of government, or actual property equity, this make-or-break role in the planning process can settle upon any or a combination of entities, including:

1. An individual or a family may own enough land to control the entire tourism planning process.

2. A company or consortium of private business organizations may have land holdings which make possible the ultimate control of resources on which plans can be based.

3. Resource-utilization decisions may reside with a governmental agency.

4. Resource-utilization decisions may be assigned to a planning commission which is limited to recommendations requiring action by a legislative body.

5. A quasi-governmental organization may be established. Such an entity, typically, would have an advisory board of governmental and, if appropriate, private-sector leaders, a working staff of its own, and some sort of official charter which empowers it to reach and implement decisions about the use of land (the critical commodity for tourism development) and other resources.

The first approach cited above can be illustrated with the situation of Costa Smeralda, located on the northeastern coast of Sardinia. A substantial parcel of real estate was assembled by a corporation in which the Aga Khan was a major figure. At the time of acquisition, the property was in its natural state, undeveloped. A single individual was able to make the commitments of land and resources necessary to develop a highly successful, integrated resort area catering to a "jet set" clientele.

The second approach described above can be illustrated with the situation in Hawaii. The commitments which made possible the post-war development boom in Hawaii were undertaken at a time when substantial portions of the resources of the island were under control of the so-called Big Five — companies controlled by a powerful group of descendants of pioneering families. Policy decisions by leaders of this homogenous group had the effect of commitments for the future of the area as a whole, particularly since there was little or no inhibiting legislation in existence at the time developmental programs were launched.

The third approach described above, under which land-use decisions reside with a governmental agency — is probably the most common. As one illustration, consider the structure established in Fiji, where town-planning boards were created at the local level. These boards have authority to commit land use. They are supported technically by the national government's town-planning division.

For the fourth approach, an example can be seen in a program currently being implemented in California. The state has a Coastal Commission responsible for studying and recommending programs for utilization of land in coastal areas. Recommendations of this group are, in turn, subject to approval and implementation by appropriate city, county, or state legislative entities.

An example of the last approach listed above can be seen in the Kovalam Beach Resort on the southwestern coast of India. A development authority was established in Kovalam as an implementation and coordinating force mobilizing private and public-sector efforts. Its activities, in turn, are interrelated with those for the state of Kerala, in which Kovalam is located, and of the national government.

THE NEED FOR A COORDINATED APPROACH TO TOURISM PLANNING

Other variations are possible. But the principle is essential: control and/or responsibiity for development of land and other resources must be vested in a decision-making entity. This entity can be an individual, a company, a specialized agency, or a coalition or coordination of entities with segmented responsibilities and authority acting together through some defined process. That is, if a single source of authority and responsibility does not exist and cannot practically be created, there must, in its stead, be a process for coordination and collaboration between the entities among which authority and responsibility are fragmented. In other words, there has to be a way of reaching decisions and taking action.

Given this capability to decide and act, the next vital ingredient for tourism planning is a process which guides and coordinates the many interrelated steps essential to tourism planning and development.

A STRUCTURED PROCESS TO ASSURE RESULTS

The anatomy of a tourism - development program assumes a predictable form. There are always variations, different features or characteristics. Overall, however, there are always recognizable patterns as well. This is inevitable. The sequence and content of activities essential to tourism development involve a number of basic common denominators. One of these has already been cited: the need for participation by individuals or entities with control over land and other critical resources. Another requirement cited in previous discussions is that it is important to identify potential markets, or origin areas, from which tourists will visit the destination under consideration.

Depending upon the detail level to which planning is carried out, a project structure can have anywhere from dozens to hundreds of activities organized into a logical, interdependent sequence. One of the obvious values in having such a structure lies in the thinking through of needs and their interrelationships which takes place. Some steps in any study and development process must precede others. There are prerequisites. There are followups. There are also many things to do, making it easy to overlook one or more activities, exposing a project to potentially costly consequences. One of the advantages of a project structure, therefore, is that it provides a checklist to be sure that basic, essential steps are taken and that these steps build upon each other with cumulative learning and documentation.

Financial considerations are also important in adopting a structured, project-management approach to tourism planning and development. Before any major attraction, facility, or destination gets into full swing, considerable expenses are encountered. By using a project structure, it becomes possible to commit funding in a series of incremental steps, or stages. At each point, investments are evaluated. In particular, early steps in the process are structured for fact finding and evaluation. The project can be terminated and its major expenses avoided on the basis of interim findings. For example, an investment of $40,000 in a feasibility study, if its findings and recommendations are negative, could save later investments in facilities which run into tens or hundreds of millions of dollars. Also avoided are the social and political commitments which can lead to embarrassing or distasteful consequences if programs fail or decisions have to be reversed because they were unsound.

In summary, a standard, structured approach to planning and development for a tourism project should make for predictability. Everyone involved knows what is to be done next, what it will cost, and the alternatives to be considered. The idea, basically is to manage the work rather than being managed by it.

PROCESS PHASES

The key steps, or phases, in a project for tourism planning and development are listed below and discussed further in the remainder of this chapter. In considering this project structure, bear in mind that the steps are defined functionally. That is, each of these phases corresponds with an event, or milestone, for the project. The duration and cost of individual phases varies widely.

The project phases are:

1. Establish Understanding
2. Preliminary Position Statement
3. Commitment for Tourism Study
4. Market and Resources Analysis
5. Conceptual Planning
6. Plan Approval
7. Master Planning
8. Final Commitment

9. Staged Implementation Program
10. Evaluation and Direction.

THE PROCESS—AN OVERVIEW

Virtually any situation in which tourism planning takes place demands an orderly series of steps which serve to establish a managerial process. With such a process, it becomes possible to coordinate the interests and activities of divergent groups. It also becomes possible to attract, appropriate, and control disbursements of the funds necessary to support tourism planning. Further, the critical decision making and program implementation requirements of a tourism program can be supported and controlled more effectively within a structured system of management.

In a sense, the remainder of this book is about such a tourism planning process. This chapter describes the steps in the process at an overview level. Succeeding chapters cover individual steps or requirements in enough depth to guide the thinking and, hopefully, the decision making necessary to tourism.

1.   Establish Understanding

A necessary first step in tourism planning is education. As logical as this may sound, it is often overlooked. Unfortunately, responsible persons have frequently faced decisions for major tourism-development programs guided chiefly by assumption or conjecture, without realizing in advance what was involved. Tourism development is a major undertaking. It has major consequences socially and economically. A frame of mind which recognizes these tremendous responsibilities and implications must be established at the outset.

As a vital, initial step, the persons who will exercise the ultimate decision power must acquire the understanding necessary to delineate a framework for their decisions. This could involve engaging lecturers or consultants for a series of presentations. It could also involve some field trips by high-level persons to areas where tourism planning and development have already taken place. Some face-to-face contact should take place between decision makers in the area, resort, or attraction considering tourism and officials from established tourism destinations. As a result of these activities, the decision makers should understand what changes they are going to be asked to approve and what the consequences of those changes are likely to be.

The first step will be of relatively short duration and involve a comparatively minor investment. Depending on the size of the group involved at the outset, the initial education can be completed in anywhere from a few weeks to a few months. Expenditures should be kept at a minimum.

This, in itself, is in keeping with principles of sound planning. That is, any effective planning process will be structured so that commitments take place one step at a time. Minimum commitments of time and funds, consistent with incremental objectives, are made at each step of the process. This leaves the planners with options for halting or altering the process at any of several established checkpoints. In each instance, decisions to halt or change courses in the planning/development cycle are based on findings and evaluations derived from the immediately preceding step. Thus, planners and decision makers get smarter by degrees. They also invest their financial and other resources on the basis of proven results as they progress.

An example of the type of support and contribution to ultimate success which can be realized from this type of early effort can be seen in the situation of Colonial Williamsburg. Before the renovation project was undertaken, extensive public meetings and education programs were held to rally the support of property owners and voters behind the appeal for the redevelopment program. Similar efforts have paid off in such areas as Hilton Head, North Carolina, and in Snowmass and Vail, in Colorado.

2.   Preliminary Position Statement

The first decision point comes right after the initial understanding is established: it is necessary to decide whether tourism development has enough potential to carry the planning effort further. If the decision is negative, the decision makers can stop at this initial point, having derived some satisfaction that they have looked at the potential and reached an intelligent decision. If they decide to proceed, they can adjust the scope and extent of their study according to their findings and opinions.

The very fact that a decision is made at this juncture leads to a requirement that the information gathered during the first phase should be documented and evaluated. The degree of detail applied in assembling this information can vary widely with the scope of the proposed project and the requirements of the persons involved. Obviously, this documentation will be more important, and should be more complete, if the key participants in this activity are favorably inclined to proceed further as they build their understanding.

If the decision is to proceed with tourism planning, the responsible group should develop a formal statement of interest. This would indicate, at an initial point, the objectives they seek and the results they wish to derive. Also important are formal, adopted statements covering any constraints upon tourism development.

At this point, the objectives and constraints can only be stated generally. But it is important that they are committed to paper and made known to all parties who will be involved. Objectives can be stated in such broad terms as the creation of new jobs, general economic goals, and limits to the degree of impacts to be tolerated upon the social customs and cultures of the area.

3.   Commitment for Tourism Study

A major necessity within any tourism-development project should be an extensive study which establishes feasibility and serves as a basis for actual development. The importance of the commitment to conduct such a study stems partly from the fact that there is a temptation, once excitement over the prospects of tourism has been generated, to abridge or minimize this activity and its importance. Once a preliminary understanding has been acquired, people with control over resources and responsibilities in an area tend to begin visualizing their properties as fully developed, complete with hotels and other attractions, and enjoying continuing streams of visitors and money.

Such temptations should be controlled, suppressed. The process of developing or expanding a tourism industry is too complex to be implemented without professional planning.

This is easily illustrated. Development of the full-scale tourism industry will require large volumes of financing. The bankers who will have to become involved in the process will require reliable data as a basis for their own commitment. These data can only result from a comprehensive study and conceptual plan which serves as a basis for application of all of the other specialties and disciplines which will have to be applied. Similarly, architects, engineers, transportation and traffic specialists, facilities planners, financial planners, and others who will have to become involved will require meaningful statements of goals and objectives as guidelines for their efforts.

The final product of this activity will be a statement of ideas and objectives presented in sufficient depth — and supported by sufficient factual data — so that a request for proposals from qualified consultants can be framed and issued. The activity comes to its conclusion with the consideration of proposals and the selection of the consulting team which will complete the next three activities in the planning process.

One comparatively recent experience in an engagement on behalf of the government of Ivory Coast, in Africa, illustrates an effective way to proceed in enunciating and moving upon this preliminary commitment. The area was already enjoying a moderate success in tourism, particularly with the French market. Government officials felt there was substantial potential for expansion. Accordingly, they developed a proposal to increase and enhance their tourism facilities. This, in turn, was taken to the World Bank for funding. The Bank, in turn, arranged for a site inspection by its lending officers. They came back with a recommendation that an impartial feasibility study be done. It was agreed that if the study led to a positive report, there was a high probability that funding would ensue. The study was commissioned at this point.

4. Market and Resources Analysis

This study activity gathers and interrelates data on the overall size of the destination's prospective market and the share of that market it can be expected to gain. Although these are two separate elements of information, one is really meaningless without the other. Therefore, the study team must interrelate its activities and findings continuously.

To illustrate, in a recent study of tourism potential in French Polynesia (particularly Tahiti) the authors started by determining, chiefly from compilations of published data, the total size of the potential market for sunshine-resort-related travel in the Pacific. This involved studies of travel patterns from places like the

United States, Japan, Australia, and elsewhere. These data presented an overall view of the total potential market.

In gathering these data, it was recognized that only a percentage of this targeted traveling population would be candidates for visitation to Tahiti and its neighboring islands. Determination of what percentage of the total market any destination will attract depends upon the related evaluation of its resources. Factors considered include:

- Cultural

- Environmental

- Recreational

- Entertainment

- Guest Facilities

- Transportation (to and within the destination area)

- Support industries

- Land availability

- Availability of suitable labor

- Capital

- Governmental attitudes.

This survey of resources serves to indicate the degree to which an area can attract a portion of the total traveling population within its region as well as its relative ability to compete for a share of both the existing and projected markets. Obviously, it is necessary to interrelate these factors to begin to draw together a body of information upon which a major investment decision and its related commitments can be based.

In performing this analysis, some data, such as travel statistics, airline routes, fare structures, and associated reports, may be readily available. Other aspects of the study require detailed review of resources in the prospective destination, as well as surveys of voyage origination, markets, the willingness of airlines to extend their routes, and other factors.

This activity involves a number of interim conclusions which become inputs to a market forecast. The market forecast, in turn, is the final product of this activity. The interim conclusions are both quantitative and qualitative in nature. Examples:

- The total potential travel to the geographic area is (or is not) great enough to support development of a tourism industry.

- Travel routes are (are not) sufficient to support development of tourism.

- The indigeneous culture in an area will (will not) serve to attract tourists.

The same type of interim conclusions are reached in connection with all the other resources cited above. Pulling these interim conclusions together and interrelating them serves to provide the basis for a forecast on the extent of tourism a prospective host area could expect to attract. This is still not a sufficient basis for a decision on whether tourism could, in fact, become viable. Knowing that a certain number of tourists can be expected is an important input to a decision on whether to proceed with tourism. But it is not, in itself, definitive. Additional studies are necessry to determine whether the area can serve this volume of tourism, whether it can build an industry to handle the influx, whether these activities will have a tolerable impact upon the social structure and customs of an area, and so on. These further considerations are covered in the next activity within the tourism planning process.

As an excellent example of market research and identification, consider the case of Sri Lanka. In 1967, the tourism revenues in this country, then known as Ceylon, were insignificant. Working with a consulting team formed by Harris, Kerr, Forster & Company, government officials evolved a concept under which potential was identified for development of the island as part of a multi-destination tour routing for trips originating in Europe and going on to Thailand. This is the kind of concept which has proved effective in identifying markets and logical development patterns.

5. Conceptual Planning

This activity starts by using outputs from the market forecast to establish the image and identification for the project area. This is done at an overall, comprehensive, but nontechnical level. That is, the entire scope of the project is encompassed in a generalized description of what the area should look like and how it will function after development has taken place.

In effect, these descriptions become a statement of policy which set the image and identification for the tourism project. Toward this end, the end items of conceptual planning include definitive statements of objectives and policies for the proposed tourism project. These deal separately with such necessary considerations as:

- The theme, or character, of the tourism project
- The major strengths or resources to be developed
- Environmental, social, and cultural aims and constraints
- Economic targets and returns.

Also dealt with during this activity are such essentials as designation of areas suitable for tourism development, guest facilities requirements, tourism attractions, land-use policies, general architectural themes, visitor movement patterns, investment policies, education and training policies, other resource commitments, and governmental policies (including a checklist of necessary legislation).

At this point, the study has produced generalized projections on potential benefits to be expected from a tourism program and the commitments that would be necessary. For both benefits and costs, figures are developed to cover only a broad range of estimates. It is still impossible to pinpoint costs or projected revenues without further planning or design. To illustrate: the survey team may be able to report that an airport will be needed, that the facility must be capable of handling large jets, and that costs can range anywhere from $10 to $15 million. Exact location and costing of such facilities will be impossible until a site-selection study is completed and engineers design the runways, determine how much earth is to be moved, establish structural and stress requirements, and so on. The same type of cost ranging can be used to project requirements in terms of roads, hotels, ground transportation, and so on.

These general estimates are close enough to give decision makers an idea of volume of tourists and revenues they can expect and the magnitude of investments and commitments which will be required. Considering the many variables of tourism planning, this kind of information represents a stepping stone. It also forms the basis for a major decision on whether to move ahead with the expensive, detailed, master planning for the actual creation of visitor facilities, or to modify, redirect, or cancel the effort.

6. Plan Approval

The important thing about this activity is to recognize its necessity. From here on, tourism planning activities become much more detailed, significantly more technical, highly sophisticated, and extremely expensive. The experience of the authors has proven, time and again, that it is really valuable to perform a conceptual planning function and to pause after it has been completed so that all parties understand, to the degree possible with rough or approximate figures, what is involved and what the likelihood of success or failure is apt to be.

Frequently, tourism surveys will plunge ahead directly from a market analysis to detailed developmental planning. The foregoing conceptual planning step is abridged to a point where it is virtually meaningless. Or it is eliminated altogether. This can be dangerous.

One of the dangers in moving ahead with the technical activities of master planning is that persons who will make the ultimate decisions can actually lose touch with what is happening in their own project. No matter how confident a group of consultants may be, they must never forget that someone else will make the decisions. Someone else's money is being spent. The customs and cultures of someone else's country or area are being impacted.

Thus, basing a decision on the best information available at this point is, at very least, highly desirable. At the same time, it would be unfair, actually impossible, to ask people to reach an extensive, definitive decision on the basis of approximated data. Thus, the decision must, necessarily, be qualified to conform to the degree of confidence which can be placed in the conceptual planning report.

Further, it must be recognized that many people, governmental officials among them, hesitate to make decisions without projections felt to be highly reliable. If the consultants performing the market analysis and conceptual planning activities hedge for their own protection, they can expect their clients to hedge in at least the same manner and degree.

Regardless of any uncertainties, however, a thorough review by responsible decision makers is so valuable that it should be considered mandatory at this point. Following this review and a specific decision on whether and to what extent the tourism planning process should proceed, master planning can take place.

7.   Master Planning

To establish a perspective for this activity, consider that master planning, typically, involves expenditures of time and money which are five to 10 *times* as extensive as all of the activities which have gone before.

Perspective also changes frequently because of the nature of cooperation required between private and public-sector entities — as well as because of the degree and extent of detailing necessary. Earlier in a project, it is easier to agree on general concepts. Now, however, specific commitments are required. This leads naturally to a division of responsibilities and interests.

This changing relationship is illustrated with the situation of airport planning, cited earlier. Conceptually, it is relatively easy to agree that tourism development requires an airport which will accommodate large jets. But when it comes to picking locations and planning facilities, responsibilities and interests tend to differ. Public-sector representatives become quickly preoccupied with land acquisition, detailing of runways, control towers, fuel storage, and other overall operational concerns. Such concerns as the design and finishing of terminals and airport hotels tend to preoccupy private-sector representatives affiliated with airlines or hotel companies. Such differences in concern frequently lead to divergence of opinions, activities, and priorities between public and private-sector personnel.

Whether or not such a divergence does emerge, it remains necessary, nonetheless, that public-sector planning go ahead into a minute level of detail for all of the elements and facilities which will provide a basis for the tourism project. For example, where a conceptual plan indicates that a certain type, class, and number of tourists can be attracted, the master plan must identify the media for reaching them and even come up with specific advertising and public-relations programs aimed at securing this business. Where a conceptual plan could indicate the need for a road connecting two given points, the master plan would include maps, structural details, and construction budgets.

Areas which should be detailed within a master plan include:

• An in-depth marketing study should be performed.
• Allocation and extent of land uses for tourism must be defined.

- Definition and planning should be completed for infrastructure facilities, including roads, airports, walkways, drainage, sewage, water, power, and other utilities.

- Sites for tourist facilities should be selected and detailed to the level of sizes and boundaries.

- Architectural design and developmental standards should be established.

- Master, overall landscape plans should be drawn.

- Zoning and other land-use regulations and controls must be established.

- Schedules or time requirements for development of tourism facilities should be detailed.

- Economic analysis and financial programming should take place. This would include detailed cost-benefit analyses.

- Investment codes, regulations, and necessary legislation should be drafted.

- Personnel development programs should be detailed. These include inventories of available skills and definitions of management and labor requirements for the area. In addition, recruiting and training programs should be planned in detail.

The situation in Sri Lanka, cited earlier as an example of effective market analysis, also carries forward as an illustration of astute master planning. A marketing study performed for this country established that the primary origin area was Europe. At the time of the study, 60 percent of visitors came from Europe. This market mix held through a growth pattern which saw an expansion of tourism of some 250 percent — from 40,000 in 1971 to 103,000 in 1975. Specific plans drawn for this area capitalized on its sun-and-sand attraction for the northern European market, Germany in particular.

Development in Sri Lanka was achieved with minimum upsets or impacts upon existing culture and natural beauty. In the experience of the authors, this is one of the most effective jobs of realistic planning and successful implementation of predefined plans encountered on the world-wide tourism scene.

8.   Final Commitment

With completion of master planning, decision makers have a detailed picture of what tourism will do to and for their area and what it should cost to achieve these results. All of these elements should be detailed to a level which makes a final decision possible.

If tourism development is to proceed, multiple commitments are necessary. The government must commit legislation, policies, funds, and programs to stimulate tourism. Bankers and other investors must commit money. Private and public-sector entities must commit to the building of hotels and other facilities.

Thus, this final commitment is complex. It must be closely coordinated. Failure to secure commitment within any sector of the new or expanded tourism industry could result in inability to implement the entire plan. Thus, master planning must recognize available and potential resources and be at a level which inspires confidence, performed by people who are experienced enough to command respect. Commitment must be irrevocable at this time or discord or strong adverse consequences can result.

9.   Staged Implementation Program

Implementation activities bridge the gap between accepted development plans and the creation of an operational, integrated tourist industry. The challenge lies chiefly in the coordination of the many elements involved. Continued planning is needed because tourism and all of its elements tend to be dynamic. It is impossible to assume that facilities and operations will materialize simply because they have been planned and the necessary funding and other resources have been committed. The evolving tourism industry must be responsive and adaptable to realities as they emerge. Thus, a staged implementation program is both an initial and a continuing need within a successful tourism project. Ultimately, implementation activities lead to creation of operational tourism facilities.

10.   Evaluation and Direction

In tourism, as in any other field, a major management challenge lies in monitoring established operations to assure continuing quality of services and operating success.

Mechanisms must be established to provide continuing feedback on volumes of tourism and levels of satisfaction provided. Such programs provide the first line of defense against decline for resorts, attractions, or destinations.

SYNOPSIS

If a tourism-development project is to succeed, a structured process should be established to provide for assurances and controls over expenses and protection for the people, customs, funds, land, and other resources involved. Such a structure applies a discipline to the necessary processes of identifying goals and objectives, building an understanding of what it will take to achieve them, and then monitoring activities to help assure success. This chapter recommends a 10-step project structure for tourism planning and development. These steps are:

1. Establish Understanding
2. Preliminary Position Statement
3. Commitment for Tourism Study
4. Market and Resources Analysis
5. Conceptual Planning
6. Plan Approval
7. Master Planning
8. Final Commitment
9. Staged Implementation Program
10. Evaluation and Direction.

REVIEW QUESTIONS

1. Why is advance planning necessary for effective tourism development?

2. What are some key advantages of a structured process for tourism planning and development?

3. Describe the differences between conceptual and master planning and explain the reasons for establishing these as separate phases.

4. Describe and illustrate the differences between the outlooks of public and private-sector managers during master planning.

5. For your area or for another with which you are familiar, describe and illustrate the values of following a structured approach for tourism development or expansion — as distinct from proceeding directly with apparently obvious expansion programs.

6. Based on what you know about your area or another, describe some specific potential pitfalls which could result from skipping or abridging a structured approach to planning.

4

GETTING
STARTED

FORMING THE INFORMATION BASE

Tourism development is a process of building. For any project, planning for tourism development will start with gathering information on things the way they are and on the potential available for desirable growth.

One of the big problems in investigating the potential of tourism can be the simple lack of information. Everybody travels. Transiency is so natural that officials in many areas, even in entire countries, have not given this phenomenon serious thought in terms of the recording of information and the development of statistics. Thus, one of the important initial steps in evaluating the potential for tourism development lies in determining present status.

This will not be as easy as it may sound. Even relatively sophisticated areas will find that tourism-related information tends to be unmeaningful or nonexistent. Information *can* exist

45

but have little or no value. For example, it is possible to have statistics on the use of hotels which do not distinguish between tourists, business visitors, local people, or transients. It is possible to have statistics on airport utilization without knowing the origins, destinations, or lengths of stay for passengers.

Even where data are available and apparently accurate, they may prove to be misleading. The authors encountered such a situation in the course of a tourism study in Malaysia. Historic records on visitor volumes showed a tenfold jump in one year, from 76,374 in 1970 to 765,232 in 1971. Taken at face value, these figures could show an apparent boom in tourism. On review and challenge, however, this apparent conclusion proved invalid. The increase occurred because of a change in rules about which visitors were counted. Before the increase, only international travelers were included. Beginning in 1971, the count encompassed all border crossings, including many thousands of persons who walked in from neighboring countries for routine daily shopping trips. In this situation, the challenge lay in identifying and separating relevant data.

Information problems may also be encountered in highly developed areas. For example, a recent study performed by Harris, Kerr, Forster & Company was aimed at overcoming information shortages on tourism in the State of California. Though the total impact of tourism on California was then estimated at some $5 billion annually, information resources necessary to guide or manage tourism as an integrated industry were all but non-existent.

In less-developed areas, the situation can be far worse than California's. Data may simply not be collected, much less reported meaningfully. Therefore, in saying that it is necessary to take stock of the current impact of tourism on an area, the authors recognize that this will not necessarily be easy or routine. Collecting meaningful, reliable data can require a major effort. The point is that the effort is worth making.

But what happens if there are no established, reliable sources? There really is no choice. Planners and investigators have to gather what data are available and do the best they can with what they have. If planning and management are to take place, some data base must be established.

Something is always available. There may be passenger statistics from airlines, steamship lines, or railroads. There may be gasoline sales tax reports as an index of highway travel. Individual resorts will have their own business records. Hotel occupancy taxes, if the area or country charges them, can be converted to some meaningful part of an information base.

This information base is a prerequisite for initiating a tourism planning program. Once assembled, this information becomes the mainstay for completing the first three phases of the project structure outlined in Chapter 3. These phases are Establish Understanding, Preliminary Position Statement, and Commitment for Tourism Study. This chapter outlines the work associated with these three phases, concluding with a description of the request for proposal (RFP) and of factors associated with selection of the vendor to perform the market analysis which constitutes the next phase of the project.

Generally, results of an initial survey will provide some pleasant surprises. Typically, the agencies or persons who control or have responsibility for land use will request information from other departments or organizations. When whatever data are available are converted to figures on revenues, employment, and impact upon the economy, the finding is generally that tourism is already bigger than anybody thought. For example, when California began to look at tourism as a single entity, it was discovered that, for many years, tourism was the second largest industry in the state, following only agriculture. Only in recent years has manufacturing — the total of all manufacturing — surpassed tourism in economic impact upon California.

This type of finding, it is worth stressing, is quite typical. Many areas have followed this route — from agriculture, to tourism, to manufacturing. This is natural because, in many instances, tourism thrives on the same basic resources as agriculture — land, sunshine, and water. Further, in the "natural" evolution from an agricultural to industrial economy, tourism plays an important economic role. Understanding of this phenomenon may be one of the important starting points for the tourism planning process in any given area. A cycle exists. In effect, one of the jobs of the tourism planners is to find out the status of their area within this natural cycle.

STATUS INFORMATION

Because tourism is an integral part of an area's economy, it is important, early in a tourism study, to relate existing tourism volumes and activities to other segments of the economy. As indicated, one typical cycle may well involve a transition from agriculture, to tourism, to industrialization. However, this is not necessarily the rule. Tourism can actually evolve from industrialization.

An understanding of the economy as a whole will help relate the needs of tourism to other developments which can be anticipated. For example, as a country develops its agriculture, a network of farm-to-market roads typically evolves. Similarly, if a country exports agricultural produce, provisions must be made for harbors, railroads, or air cargo. All of these capabilities bear upon tourism.

Studying these figures will also provide a perspective for the decision makers. Suppose, for example, an area with a moderate climate and an abundant supply of water is predominantly agricultural at the moment. The area has a river basin, several lakes, and some seashore. There is a thriving truck-farming industry for local consumption as well as an established export trade centering around timber and two cash crops. Labor utilization is low, with unemployment running at approximately 20 percent, as close as anybody can tell.

A neighboring country has built tourism into its major industry. However, governmental officials and citizens in this area are concerned about the urbanization, slum conditions, and pollution which affected their neighbor following rapid economic development.

The government in this developing area is in a position to control land use through zoning legislation. The government could condemn and acquire land if necessary. Officials, however, would prefer to present a definitive developmental plan and seek voluntary cooperation by both private individuals and businesses.

A logical starting point here would be for the government to set up an information-gathering task force. Domestic economic data collected would include hotel revenues, hotel occupancy rates, air and other travel statistics, foreign currency exchange data, import-export volume and commodity figures, and other financially relevant information. In addition, the data-gathering group would also be asked to report on labor availability, readiness of the people to accept the impact of tourism, and readiness of the financial and business establishments in the area to expand and support tourism activities.

This group would also look at the land resources, roads, travel facilities, and potential attractions within its own area. Also considered would be climate, including such seasonal factors as temperature, rainfall, wind, humidity, snowfall, and projected average days of sunshine. All of these elements would be included in the section of the group's report covering resources and prospects for the area.

LOOKING OUTWARD

If a tourism program is to succeed, it needs a market which can be created or tapped. Tourism can develop under three different types, or sets, of conditions:

1. The region already has a thriving tourism industry and a potential new destination wishes to acquire a share of the market.

2. A nearby market exists. Building a tourism destination under this condition would involve extending that market.

3. Creation of a tourism destination would mean building entirely new markets, travel patterns, and so on.

To illustrate the first type of situation, consider the activities of Aruba in seeking a share of the Caribbean market or San Diego in attempting to enlarge its share of the Southern California tourism industry.

For an illustration of the second situation, consider attempts by areas like Fiji or Tahiti to attract visitors who extend Pacific area travel plans. Similarly, the neighbor island of Hawaii built its tourism business by tapping into the existing Honolulu market.

Possibly the outstanding current example of the third type of situation lies in programs announced recently by the Soviet Union for a trade center in Moscow and for enhancement of travel and hotel accommodations throughout the country. The opening of mainland China to outside travel also illustrates a major activity triggered by recognition of the economic potential of tourism.

Each of these types of situations calls for different degrees or levels of commitment in building a market. But there are also common denominators. Transportation routes are essential. They must either exist or be created. Similarly, airport facilities must be created or adapted. Hotels and attractions for visitors must also be opened or expanded.

Determining the position and requirements of an area moving into tourism is not as difficult as might be assumed. As strange as it may seem, there are more statistics of a more reliable nature available on international and regional travel than there are in most individual countries. These information resources include:

- The World Tourism Organization (WTO), headquartered in Geneva, publishes extensive statistics on international travel. This organization also has some valuable publications aimed at guiding tourism development.

- The Organization for Economic Cooperation and Development (OECD) assembles, publishes, and distributes extensive economic data on the so-called western countries. This organization has pioneered in the inclusion of tourism in economic analyses.

- A number of regional travel and tourism organizations have been formed to promote tourism of member countries. In support of these activities, travel and tourism data are collected and distributed widely. Typical of such organizations are the Pacific Area Travel Association (PATA), the European Travel Commission (ETC), and the Caribbean Travel Association (CTA).

- The International Air Travel Association (IATA) publishes highly reliable figures on international air travel.

- The Travel Research Association (TTRA) is a source of information on United States and international tourism trends.

- A number of international organizations are active in the tourism area. Included are the World Bank, the International Bank for Reconstruction and Development, the United Nations Development Program, the Asian Bank, the Overseas Private Investment Corporation (OPIC, a U.S. government corporation), and the Inter-American Development Bank (IADB).

- The United States Travel Service (USTS), part of the U.S. Department of Commerce, provides annual statistics on travel to the United States from other countries and from the United States by U.S. residents.

- In the private sector, Harris, Kerr, Forster & Company and others publish annual statistical studies on hotel occupancy.

- Many tourism studies completed for governments or foundations are now in the public domain and may provide useful references.

Many other sources exist, but these illustrate the point. In examining the potential of tourism, it is essential to look outward as well as inward. In the hypothetical area described earlier, the data-gathering team would contact these and other organizations, accumulating data on existing markets which a tourism industry in the area could tap into as well as potential new sources of tourism revenue which could be cultivated.

Activities of the data gatherers would also include some financial soundings. They would make it known to leading banks and investors inside and outside their own country that tourism development was being considered. Responses indicating willingness to invest, prospective interest rates for borrowing, the willingness of hotel chains to put up facilities in the area, the ability of international airlines to extend routes or increase frequency of service, and other readily attainable responses all serve to bear upon a preliminary picture of market and financial feasibility.

PROJECTING REQUIREMENTS

Once data have been gathered, the next challenge for the study group lies in reducing it to meaningful reports. The process is partially one of interpretation. Statistics and operating data on the domestic economy and on tourism and finance from elsewhere must be correlated. The idea is to focus their meaning in terms of the specific decision to be made. These projections should also evaluate and describe the degree of reliability attributed to data used for conclusions and projections.

Content of reports should be varied according to needs of users. For example, the chief executive of a country might need only a general summary to approve a recommendation. However, the ministers making the recommendation would need to satisfy themselves on the probable impacts of development alternatives in terms of the economy, projected revenues, culture, customs, and so on. Persons reporting to the ministers, in turn, would need increasing levels of detail.

At each level, it is important that the implications of the information be understood and that consequences of decisions be made clear for all participants. If the tourism-development decision is affirmative, the destination is committed to extensive change. Therefore, it is imperative in assembling statistics, reports, and recommendations that all involved parties understand what they are seeing and have enough information to reach the incremental decisions involved. At this initial phase of a tourism study, the commitment requested is a determination on whether to proceed with more extensive conceptual planning. With each positive decision, it should be understood, the likelihood of proceeding with the tourism-development project increases.

ASSURING UNDERSTANDING

It is important that the authorities who control land-use decisions understand the implications of a decision to proceed with a major tourism study. At this point, the idea is to comprehend the interrelationships of the area, the people, and the financial commitments involved.

The need for understanding stems largely from the fact that tourism development requires high levels of commitment and investment, as compared with other industries, before significant revenues are realized. The patterns for typical private-sector and public-sector investment in a new tourism industry are shown schematically in Figure 4-1. For both the public and private sectors, cumulative expenditures mount rapidly, with no revenues realized until just prior to the heaviest point of financial commitment.

In the case of public-sector investments, development of infrastructure requirements such as roads, utilities, and facilities is well along before initial revenues are realized from private-sector payments for land leases and property taxes. Similarly, private-sector development is nearing completion before initial revenues from tourism take place.

Economic payout for investments by public and private-sector entities are covered in a later chapter. At the outset, however, the pattern of investment and return should be known to all parties. There are investment opportunities which involve faster turnaround than tourism. Persons not extensively experienced in tourism investment and operations should understand this clearly and early. Many tourism ventures have failed for no other reason than a lack of understanding about financial return.

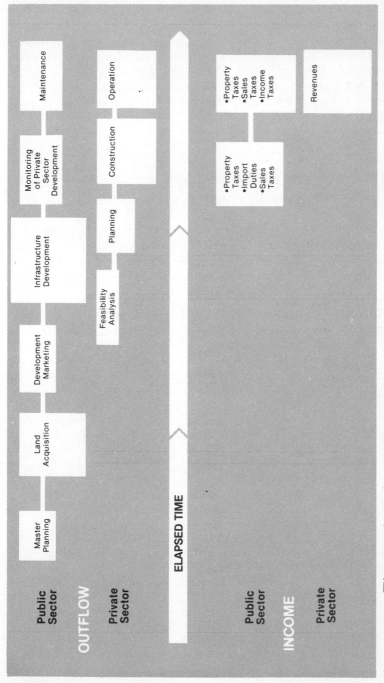

Figure 4-1. Time-related relationships between investment requirements and revenue expectations in tourism development.

Any entity undertaking a tourism investment must be able to carry itself long enough to realize projected returns. This could take years. The point: in any undertaking of this magnitude there will be divisions of responsibilities between persons who gather, interpret, and make decisions on the basis of data. Procedures must be established to assure that understanding takes place at every level. The end result of all this activity will be a major, costly decision. The more reliable the information on which the decision is based and the better it is understood by all parties, the greater the chances for success.

ESTABLISHING OBJECTIVES

Initially gathered data should develop a composite picture of what tourism can do for and to an area. To relate these projected results to a decision on whether to proceed with tourism development, there must be a basis for comparison. This basis is the cumulative set of objectives which should be developed concurrently with the gathering, reduction, evaluation, and presentation of information on tourism potential.

Basically, objectives for tourism should be a subset of the overall objectives (either implicit or documented) for the government, the economy, the people, and the social structure within an area. There may be cases in which serious consideration of the potential of tourism forces evaluation of where national or area objectives probably are, even though these may not actually be documented. At best, there are no hard, firm rules about what objectives should be. In general, however, tourism-study objectives should deal with:

- Growth
- Standard of living
- Culture and customs
- Employment levels
- Opportunities for intellectual growth
- Recognition on the international scene
- Enhancement of the investment potential in an area or country.

Cumulatively, tourism objectives should describe the set of conditions under which a favorable decision would be made. If the information projection does not come up to these expectations, the decision would be negative. If the expectations are met or exceeded, the decision makers would probably proceed unless other adverse consequences come to light.

SEEKING ASSISTANCE

If data indicate that reasonable objectives for tourism development can be met, this will generally lead to a decision to proceed with a conceptual planning study. This will generally be done by seeking assistance from outside, objective consultants. This is the most likely method for securing the needed expertise for comparatively short periods and also for assuring the objectivity demanded by international lenders.

To illustrate, the following generalized objectives are condensed from a set used recently in a tourism study for a growing Pacific area destination:

- Develop a tourism industry which, in all aspects and at all levels, is of high quality, though not necessarily of high cost.
- Encourage the use of tourism for both cultural and economic exchange.
- Distribute the economic benefits of tourism, both direct and indirect, as widely and to as many of our citizens as feasible.
- Preserve our cultural and natural resources as part of tourism development. Facilitate this through architectural and landscape design which reflect our traditions.
- Appeal to a broad cross-section of international and domestic tourists through policies and programs of site and facility development.

As a basis for moving ahead with the conceptual planning study, a request for proposal (RFP) should be prepared. This is a description and set of guidelines for the study which will be used by prospective consulting organizations (vendors) as a uniform basis for submitting proposals.

In preparing an RFP, a local entity can be guided by many similar documents which have been prepared in the past. Copies of these will generally be available through international organizations involved in tourism development, such as the World Bank or the World Travel Organization. Regional travel associations should also be able to provide specimens.

To illustrate the scope of the work involved, the following is a topical outline adapted from an actual RFP used in connection with the same program for which objectives were cited earlier:

I.   *Conceptual Plan*
     Market Analysis
     Area and Land Use
     Transportation and Infrastructure Requirements
     Accommodations and Related Facilities Requirements
     Economic Evaluation

II. *Administrative and Management Implementation Plan*
     The Tourism Organization
     Zoning and Building Code Requirements
     Schedule for Development and Capital Needs
     Education and Training Plan
     Transportation and Infrastructure Development Plan
     Architectural and Landscaping Plans

III. *Consultant's Plan of Work*

IV. *Consultant's Statements of Qualifications*

V.   *Fees*

VI. *Staffing of Engagement and Qualifications of Individuals*

A document built upon such an outline serves to establish a logical, workable sequence and organization for conduct of the conceptual planning study — and for evaluation of proposals. In the first section, the RFP provides a description of tasks to be performed in establishing a conceptual overview of a project. The identified tasks begin with a market analysis and proceed through other general requirements (covered in later chapters of this book) to produce an economic evaluation of prospects.

Typically, the project would be checkpointed after preparation of the economic evaluation. At this juncture, the consultants should be able to provide an appraisal, based on their expertise and experience, on whether the proposed project is feasible. If so, the study can proceed into the next phase.

The second section of the RFP asks the consultants to develop a plan for managing, on an integrated basis, the development of the tourism project. In this section, the vendor tells the client what will have to be done to proceed with detailed master planning and actual development of the destination.

In the remaining sections, the consultants are asked to outline how they would proceed if awarded the contract, describe their qualifications, quote fees, and identify the people who would conduct the study, giving their qualifications.

After proposals have been received, the RFP provides a set of standards against which they can be measured. There may be wide variations in the approaches taken, the work to be done, the people to be assigned, and, inevitably, in prices quoted.

For example, in presenting a plan of work for the engagement, each bidder should demonstrate a broad range of background and skills. Consider such diverse topics as projections of visitor resources; planning for visitor attractions; organization; manpower development; economic analyses; the setting of investment criteria and standards, and the others. If proposals are weighed critically, the evaluators will be able to determine whether each organization has the necessary skills and experience and in what depth. To perform a tourism survey, any organization should have persons available for such diverse skills as marketing, research and analysis, economics, statistics, accounting, finance, architecture, engineering, demographics, natural resources, meteorology, and so on. Without sufficient breadth or depth, something will suffer.

At best, a consultant's recommendation on tourism planning will be highly subjective. No recommendation can be any better than the background, the experience, the practices, and the capabilities of the people who do the work. Therefore, statements of qualifications incorporated in an RFP should be weighed competitively.

Proposed fees are important. But they may not be the determining factor in the acceptance or rejection of any given proposal. Occasionally, governmental agencies stipulate an outside limit or budget for a study. This can be helpful. But proposals received will still vary widely in fees quoted. Fee differentials should be considered in light of the appropriateness of efforts, disciplines, and capabilities to be applied.

In evaluating proposals, decision makers should also consider whether the work is being done by a single organization or a consortium of firms who have joined together for this proposal. If multiple organizations are invovled in a single bid, it is important to know where responsibility resides. It is valuable to know whether the organizations which have pooled their resources for this bid have worked together before and what their track record has been. A good technique is to ask the bidders who will perform the study to whom questions or complaints can be referred, and where responsibility will reside.

AWARDING THE CONTRACT

The awarding of a contract for a tourism study represents a major milestone. The award carries with it the delegation of responsibilities and authority to act on behalf of the responsible entity. As in any management situation, however, full authority and responsibility are never relinquished. Persons with ultimate responsibility for land use in their area should be cognizant enough of what is happening in the conceptual planning study to monitor and evaluate results, both intermittently and at the conclusion of the project. The chapters which follow will deal with individual, critical aspects of tourism studies.

SYNOPSIS

The first step in determining whether a tourism development or expansion program is advisable is to gather information on potential opportunities and pitfalls. When evaluated, this information provides the basis for a decision on whether to proceed with formal planning or to delay, abort, or modify the program. Both internal and external data on tourism activities affecting the area under consideration should be assembled. This task should use published statistics on travel and tourism which are readily available from international and regional organizations. In addition, travel and accommodations statistics should be assembled from the region under study. Data specifically applicable to an individual tourism-development project may be hard to find. But efforts should be made to pull together everything available, then to weigh and evaluate reliability of information as part of the decision on whether to proceed with the project. Concurrently with the gathering of data, decision makers responsible for the project should also consider the objectives for tourism development. These objectives and supporting descriptions should be incorporated in a preliminary position statement which provides the basis for a decision on whether to proceed further with the tourism program. If this decision is affirmative, the logical next step is to prepare a request for proposal (RFP), which is distributed to consulting organizations which are prospective bidders for a contract to perform a conceptual planning study. The materials in this chapter cover the first three phases of the structured tourism-development process outlined in Chapter 3. These phases are Establish Understanding, Preliminary Position Statement, and Commitment for Tourism Study.

REVIEW QUESTIONS

1. Describe some of the information-gathering difficulties which could be anticipated in preparing a preliminary position report on any tourism destination with which you are personally familiar.

2. Explain the relationship between reliability of data about a destination's prospects and the financing of a tourism development program.

3. Prepare a preliminary draft of a statement of objectives for a tourism area with which you are familiar, paying particular attention to setting objectives associated with the preservation of customs, culture, and natural resources.

4. Review the outline in this chapter covering an RFP for a conceptual planning study. Applying this outline to a destination with which you are familiar, write a brief (one page) description of scope for a marketing study for that area.

5

MARKET AND RESOURCES ANALYSIS

ESTABLISH MARKET POSITION

An important, early step in establishing a tourism destination or attraction lies in identifying what the area has to sell — or what needs to be done to develop saleability. Putting it another way, it is important to put together a thorough, comprehensive inventory of the elements which comprise the image of an area in its marketplace. This should include both strengths and weaknesses.

In general, the strengths will be apparent to persons associated with an area. For example, an attractive beach, a warm climate, rolling surf, museums or visitor centers, or cultural affinities for an identified market will speak for themselves. Less apparent is the process of challenging the total experience of the tourist to find voids or shortcomings. For example, a given resort area may have a world-renowned golf course. But it may fail to meet its full potential as the hub of a tourims industry because of a lack of first-class restaurants, nightclubs, or theatres where guests can be entertained in the evening.

In building a tourism destination, a successful vacation can be likened to a honeymoon: the people and the place must be meant for each other if the tourists are to realize a happy experience. Similarly, the facilities, the commitment, and the operation of the destination must be attractive and enjoyable for visitors.

Just as there are types of people who gravitate toward each other, so also are there types of tourism areas and attractions which lure different categories of travelers. As a starting point, therefore, a market analysis should identify basic strengths or appeals. The purpose is to build an understanding of what general type of appeal an area will provide and what type of tourists it is apt to attract.

Broadly, tourism areas or attractions fall into two general categories:

1. Destinations
2. Stopovers.

A *destination* is an area with sufficient attraction to provide primary motivation for tourism visits. Further, a destination will have a broad enough base of activities and interests to occupy the tourists for several days, possibly weeks. Beach-type resorts, urban areas with a wide assortment of things to do, or areas which feature gaming casinos are prime examples of destinations.

Stopovers are necessary or interesting places to visit on the way to destinations. Stopovers tend to build tourism volume on the basis of historical, cultural, architectural, or commercial attractions which hold tourists' interest for a day or two. Examples range from shopping trips to Hong Kong, to the battlefield at Gettysburg, to the pyramids and archeological findings in the Yucatan or southern regions of Mexico.

Certain areas, such as Tahiti, can be both destinations and stopovers. Tahiti and the Society Islands chain embody the attractions necessary to maintain the tourist's interest for several days. In addition, because of its geographic location almost midway between Sydney and Los Angeles, Tahiti is also a convenient stopping place to break the 20-hour trip between North America and Australia.

Areas with such characteristics can also be regarded as *secondary destinations.*

Focal points of tourism activity or interest within either destinations or stopovers are generally referred to as *attractions.* A typical attraction will provide between one-half and two days of tourism experience. Some typical attractions are natural or historic landmarks, museums, or amusement and recreation facilities.

In starting a market study, it is a good idea to identify the area or property as a destination or stopover. This is best done by looking at the sum of attractions available from the viewpoint of the prospective tourist following identified, established travel patterns. It is not difficult to simulate a typical tourist's experience in terms of interests and attention spans. This process is invaluable in establishing a basis for market planning. End results of this first step should be an understanding of what the area will mean to the experience of future tourists and what length of stay can be anticipated.

TAKE STOCK

After targeting prospects, it is important to gather information on where the area or property is at the moment. Almost anyplace, today, will have some tourism traffic. If an area or proposed facility is in a continental location which experiences substantial interregional traffic, the best method for determining current tourism volumes will be to check with hotels. Even raw statistics on hotel occupancy will provide an idea of how many out-of-town persons stay in an area, for how long. If better statistics are available, it may be possible to differentiate between tours, independent tourists, and business visitors. Statistics from airlines and other carriers may also be helpful.

If the area happens to be an island or an independent country, meaningful data may be available from statistics on entry and departure (E/D). In conjunction with the issuing of E/D cards, some countries routinely ask questions about origin, destination, length of stay, and so on. In other situations, samplings of visitors are asked to complete questionnaires as they pass through customs or as they arrive and depart.

Any of these techniques, or all in combination, should be designed to produce the same results: a profile of the current tourist and tourism volumes. As indicated earlier, most organizations conducting this type of study find themselves pleasantly surprised. In most places, tourism proves to be larger than anticipated.

DATA REQUIREMENTS

In general, two different sets of data should be accumulated. One set, typically, is gathered from hotels, carriers, immigration authorities, and other institutional sources. The other is elicited from tourists themselves.

Tourism market statistics gathered from industry sources should include:

- Number of visitors
- Seasonality or seasonal patterns of visits
- Origination points
- Destination points
- Length of stay
- Reason for visit
- Attractions visited
- Services used in the destination or stopover area.

Statistics gathered from tourists themselves should include:

- Age range of visitors
- Party size
- Mode of transportation
- Income level
- Occupation
- An approximation of spending in the area
- First-time or repeat visit incidence
- Group or individual travel
- Satisfaction level.

DETERMINE THE SITUATION

Building upon data already assembled, the next step is to gather statistics on tourism markets and to identify those with the greatest potential. This is done by looking at publicly available statistics and evaluating them in light of the growing knowledge of the area under study.

The primary objective at this point is to determine origin points of prospective visitors.

Thus, the profile and market analysis data described above can be matched against world markets to identify growth potential.

In general, the factors affecting probabilities of attracting tourists from any given, identified market will include:

- Distance
- Time
- Cost of getting to and staying in an area
- Cultural ties
- Propensity to travel
- Educational opportunities
- Established reputation among travelers and travel professionals
- Security.

These factors are not absolute or clear cut in their application. On the one hand, for example, the islands in the Caribbean have built a substantial tourism business by capitalizing on the factors of distance, time, and cost because of proximity to their primary markets. However, this does not say that these factors are necessarily primary. The strong, traditional European tourism business derived from the United States market is based heavily on cultural ties and propensity of U.S. citizens to travel to the lands of their roots.

Examples of tourism industries built largely on cultural ties which override the factors of travel time and cost can be seen in the continuing flow of visitors to Israel, the growing number of visitors to Africa, and, in large measure, the Japanese tourist industry.

In general, this phase of the study will be aimed at determining where potential markets lie and what share can be captured by the area under study. This is done chiefly by correlating the data on the profile of visitors currently attracted with data on travel patterns from their areas of origin. There may also be major markets to examine for potential regardless of existing patterns. It is no secret, for instance, that the United States is the largest tourist source market in the world. However, many successful resort areas have been built and have thrived by serving tourists from such areas as Germany, Japan, the Scandinavian countries, and elsewhere. Tourism is a long-range investment. In performing a tourism survey, all feasible potential should be reviewed.

EASE OF TOURIST MOVEMENT

Although it is necessary to secure and tabulate certain basic data, this work must be done as unobtrusively as possible. After long and arduous travel, the tourist is annoyed by government requirements. If surveys become annoyances, tourists can receive an unfavorable initial impression of the host country or area.

The same is true on exit requirements. Again, although certain data must be collected to maintain accurate records on tourism, encroachment on pleasure travel must be minimized.

As another consideration, customs officials, both on entry and exit, must be courteous and should be multilingual if appropriate. One thing that can be done is to train customs inspectors to apologize while explaining the necessity for what they are doing. To illustrate, an example of a negative operation of this type was encountered not long ago at New Delhi's international airport. Customs officials were conducting exit examinations to determine whether Indian nationals and possibly tourists were leaving the country with illegal amounts of currency or gold. Although this is a necessary government procedure, it would be more advisable to segregate the tourist from the Indian national.

ANALYZE ATTRACTIONS

Concurrently with analyzing market potential, it is important to take an objective, calculating look at attractions in the area and develop realistic estimates of their potential for attracting tourists. This phase of the market study has two basic parts:

1. Inventory the attractions.

2. Evaluate their potential.

The inventorying task is straightforward. The job is to take stock of existing or potential attractions, including beaches, mountains, lakes, hunting preserves, museums, or unspoiled natural areas.

Listing of attractions should be done inclusively; evaluation of the items must be handled objectively. It isn't enough simply to say that there is a beach. There should also be descriptions covering seasonal water temperature, quality of swimming, surf and tides, accessibility, natural vegetation, or other factors. For example, there are many potentially great beaches with swimming areas choked by coral. In other areas, sandbars restrict swimming; in still others, kelp beds make bathing uncomfortable. Further, the announced presence of or threats from sharks, stone fish, barracuda, or men o'war can negate the allure of otherwise attractive beaches. It could also be important to know whether beaches lend themselves to surfing, the fishing conditions, and so on.

Beaches are, of course, just an example, the idea is to gather enough data for evaluations on whether attractions will interest prospective tourists. The nature and extent of the descriptions should be geared to the nature of the prospective tourists who have been identified. For example, a resort featuring sunshine and beaches will, in most cases, depend upon a nearby volume market. Conversely, sport fishing or big-game hunting do not depend on market proximity. The same people are equally apt to be interested in an African safari or a Kodiak bear hunt in Alaska. The same people are just as apt to be interested in sport fishing off New Zealand as they are in the Caribbean. Archeological attractions also tend to be geographically independent of origin markets. Similarly, cultural attractions will transcend the conveniences of time and distance.

Also to be inventoried at this point are the social, political, natural, and attitudinal assets. Obviously, for example, if the area is populated by friendly people who will welcome visitors and show them friendship, this is an asset. Just as obviously, racial or political tension will become a liability very quickly. A change in the attitudes of local residents will lead to noticeable differences in tourism patterns. This has been quite apparent in the changing travel patterns experienced by some of the island republics in the Caribbean.

In studying market potential, the prospects for local and domestic visitors to tourism attractions should be weighed carefully. In either isolated or metropolitan areas, local residents account for a considerable portion of visitor volumes at attractions.

RESOURCES CHECKLIST

The resources of an area which may be inventoried for analysis as tourist attractions, or as necessary building blocks for a tourism industry, can include:

- Cultural/historical attributes
- Environmental
- Recreational
- Entertainment
- Shopping and dining
- Architecture
- Climate and other natural resources
- Transportation
- Support industries
- Land
- Labor force
- Capital
- Governmental attitudes.

These resource categories fall naturally into two broad groupings. The first, encompassed by the initial seven types of resources identified above, is associated with the marketing image projected by an area, a resort, or a facility. That is, these items, collectively, are directly associated with the attraction of tourists into an area. Thus, their appeal is external. Their degree of necessity varies according to related strengths and weaknesses of the individual resorts or attractions.

The remaining six categories of resources listed above are operational, or functional, in nature. That is, these are the things which must be present if tourists are to be accommodated and served. They are necessities, even though they may play no direct role in bringing tourists into an area or entertaining them.

Each of these inventory items has special requirements and presents special challenges of its own, as discussed below.

Cultural/Historical Attributes

Studying culture and heritage objectively can be challenging, even difficult. Where a tourism market study is concerned, however, it is important to recognize that customs and culture may be part of the product offered. Cultural attractions can be direct or indirect. That is, there can be a substantial market of persons with cultural ties to an area. This is evidenced by visits to Ireland by U.S. residents of Irish descent, the substantial tourism industry in Israel which attracts Jews from around the world, visits by Japanese descendants to Japan, black Americans to Africa, and so on.

In addition, there can be a strong attraction of people from highly industrialized areas to places with calm, unsophisticated lifestyles. This, for example, proved a factor in the evaluation of the tourism potential in Fiji.

Cultural and historical events can also provide strong tourism attractions. A dramatic example of a specific culturally related event which has become the foundation of a strong tourism volume is the New Orleans' *Mardi Gras*. Other fiestas and special holidays have been similarly attractive. Consider, for example, the *Oktoberfest* in Germany and *Cinco de Mayo* in Mexico.

Thus, it could be profitable to consider holidays or events which could provide special attraction for tourists. However, such potential should be evaluated carefully. If successful, such promotions or observances tend to bring in peak loads of tourism activity for short periods. This could have its drawbacks as well as its potential advantages. If such promotions are considered, thought should be given also to the potential damage of turning down reservations or having tourists disappointed by over-crowded conditions.

A different, perhaps steadier type of appeal may develop around historical, archeological, religious, or cultural sites. These can range widely. Certainly, Greece has built the major portion of its tourism around the ruins of its ancient civilization. The same, to some degree, is true in Italy, Mexico, the Middle East, and other areas.

Such locations can serve either as primary or secondary attractions. The number and concentration of such sites can bear upon the level of attraction. For example, the fact that Greece has an entire ancient civilization in a concentrated area represents a major attraction. Conversely, the Tower of London or Notre Dame Cathedral, while they are landmarks of the first magnitude, really play auxiliary roles as tourism attractions. Similarly, few tourists build their entire vacation plans around Mt. Vernon, in Virginia. However, this historic landmark is an important attraction for visitors to nearby Washington, D.C., Williamsburg, Monticello, and other historical and cultural attractions in the area.

Objectivity is especially important in studying culture as a tourist attraction. It can be hard for people indigenous to an area to understand or appreciate the attraction of their culture to others. A qualified observer familiar with the market in tourism-origin areas should be involved in these evaluations.

Environmental Considerations

This part of the survey can also profit from objectivity. The idea is to look at all of the attractions, settings, or sites of natural beauty which might attract visitors. A resource could be as simple as clean air. For example, some areas in the mountains around Denver thrive on the attraction of their respiratory conditions for city dwellers. The attraction could be recreational, such as skiing, water sports, shooting rapids, or other experiential drawing cards. There are also beaches, rivers, lakes, forests, terrain which lends itself to golf, and so on.

It is worth stressing that though detailed studies are not performed at this point, qualifications and experience of the survey-team members are important. It may not be necessary to call in a golf course architect at this point. But a person experienced in evaluating and working with golf resorts will know potential for suitable terrain.

It may be necessary, however, to arrange for the early presence of experts qualified to prepare environmental impact statements on resources which could be affected by a tourism program. If environmental impact legislation is in force, it may well be mandatory to include statements in reports covering conceptual plans for tourism development. Political and legislative controls over use of environmental resources are assuming worldwide proportions.

Recreational Areas and Facilities

This part of the survey can be closely associated with the study of environmental considerations. In the environmental area, there is potential. In the recreational area, there are existing facilities. If large-scale recreational facilities already exist, the chances are that a tourism industry is well along toward formation or development. Should this be the case, there will probably be available skills in the area for evaluating potential.

Studies and evaluations of recreational attractions should identify the category into which each fits. Two broad categories of recreational attraction should be used: general and unique. General facilities are universal in appeal. Examples include skiing, golf, tennis, swimming, or surfing. Unique attractions are specific to one or a few areas. Examples include safaris, big game hunting, game fishing, bullfighting, or dude ranching.

Entertainment

Entertainment is different from recreation in the context used here. Entertainment can be either the main attraction for certain classes of tourists, or it can be supportive for the overall tourism industry in an area.

To be a primary attraction, entertainment should be unique in scope or scale. For example, Shakespeare festivals in Stratford, Connecticut; San Diego, California, and Medford, Oregon, draw sizeable numbers of people specifically to see performances of proven theatrical merit. An example of supportive entertainment can be seen in Las Vegas and Reno, Nevada. People are attracted by casino gaming but have come to expect lavish cabaret-type shows as added attractions.

In some urban areas, theatrical industries provide tourism attractions. On the west coast, Universal City and other movie-studio tours serve as supporting attractions. In New York City and London, the theatrical districts provide attractions for many devotees.

Local entertainment can be an important supplement to resort areas which sell relaxation primarily. The age-old question is: "What do you do around here at night?" There are many resorts which feature golf, swimming, surfing, and other daytime-oriented specialties which attract people who like to fill their evenings with dancing, dining, drinking, and some cabaret-type entertainment. At least some availability of such entertainment can make a difference. Certainly, such facilities should be considered in inventorying prospective tourism resources.

Shopping and Dining

A high proportion of tourists are compulsive shoppers and/or cuisine samplers. They visit everything from local fish markets, to flower markets, to supermarkets, to fashionable boulevards or massive regional shopping complexes. Depending on tastes, they devour familiar food, local delicacies, or both.

Attraction value of shopping facilities will be based on uniqueness, variety, or price. The attraction of free ports such as Hong Kong is a good example. Another example is the development of St. Thomas, which draws heavily from the Puerto Rican tourist trade as a shopping haven for bargain hunters. Similarly, tourists are attracted regularly to areas such as Carneby Street in London, Fifth Avenue in New York, Michigan Avenue in Chicago, and others.

Specialty areas such as Ghiaradelli Square or The Cannery in San Francisco or Cannery Row in Monterey, California, have built popularity by combining opportunities for shopping and dining.

In some instances, demands for unique art and handicraft styles of an area have led to development of substantial industries for manufacturing and marketing specialty items. An example can be seen in the substantial numbers of replicas of Mayan or Aztec sculptures and decorative items made and sold in Mexico. The same themes have also carried over into related crafts, such as textiles and leather goods. Another illustration of the same potential can be seen in the hundreds of thousands of items of coral and sea-shell jewelry sold annually in Hawaii. In Japan, tourists have collected many of the same items of dinnerware and flatware which are commonly used in local homes.

The point: tourists regularly budget substantial amounts of their vacation money for shopping and dining. Providing facilities to accommodate these interests serves both to build the attraction potential of an area and also to enhance revenues.

Architectural Attractions

In the minds of many tourists, and certainly in the content of promotion which builds tourism industries, architectural landmarks have frequently become symbolic of the areas in which they are located. This is easy to illustrate:

- San Francisco is closely associated with the Golden Gate Bridge.
- New York has its Statue of Liberty, Empire State Building, and Radio City.
- London has Buckingham Palace.
- Rome has the Vatican.
- The Eiffel Tower is synonymous with Paris.
- India has the Taj Majal.

- Sydney has its Opera House.
- Pisa has its leaning tower.

Other examples abound. Clearly, it can be profitable, during a tourism market survey, to consider existing architectural landmarks and to think about future plans or opportunities in this direction.

Climate and Other Natural Resources

Climate, water temperature, surf, snow, wind, or more recently, air and water pollution can be make-or-break factors affecting the success of a tourism industry. In particular, a tourism survey should concentrate on seasonality of climate and other natural conditions. This is particularly critical for areas with outdoor-oriented attractions. Ultimately, a determination of whether tourism is feasible for an area will center around projections of numbers of visitors and cash flow they will generate. Obviously, the longer the season a prospective tourism industry will enjoy, the better its economic picture will look.

Transportation

Transportation is an area which requires considerable attention and emphasis. Without transportation, there is simply no tourism. Even at an early stage in a tourism survey, therefore, it is important to look at transportation situations and requirements with some breadth and depth.

One dimension of review should cover both existing and potential expansion requirements for an area's transportation network. In another dimension, the survey should review transportation to and from the area as well as within the region.

Concerns and information needs center around several aspects of transportation, including:

- Be aware of existing forms of transportation and their adequacy. It is not enough, for example, to find that there is an expandable airport facility. If the airport does expand, how will the increased ground traffic be handled? Will special roads be needed? Will it be necessary to build or expand rail transportation capabilities? Will it be necessary to add bus routes? If so, what will this do to street traffic?

- Consider time-zone constraints which may apply. People generally prefer departure times convenient to their normal life styles and schedules. These should be related to prospective arrival times in the destination area — as well as the impact of schedules upon prospective tourists.

- Consider existing schedules. Are they adequate? Will increases or time adjustments be necessary? Are projected demands reasonable and potentially profitable for the carriers involved?

- Consider existing travel routes. Do they provide adequate accessibility from primary and secondary markets? If not, what changes would be necessary?

- How does the cost of traveling to the area compare with other areas trying to attract the same tourists? Apply this comparison to excursion and group fares as well as to standard rates.

Tourism is all about getting someplace else. Capabilities to move people comfortably and competitively are essentials for success.

Support Industries

If tourism is to take hold and grow, it needs to be nurtured and supported. An entire network of what amount to life-support systems for the tourism industry must either exist or be created.

Requirements range all the way from taxi and bus service, to complete agricultural and food supply capabilities, to construction, to manufacturing of construction and supply items, to distributing liquors and beverages, to foreign currency exchange, to telephone and other utility services, to a wide range of professional activities. Professional requirements include medical care, marketing, accounting, law, architecture, engineering, and general management.

In a highly industrialized area, such support capabilities are apt to prove little or no problem. However, in a developing area, support industries can present major challenges. Where a country or area does not have all of the professional and operational capabilities needed to support tourism, major decisions must be faced. These include determinations on whether:

- Sufficient talents and capabilities are in place and available

- There is time and capability for training and building support requirements which may not already exist

- Immigration and customs regulations are to be relaxed to permit importation of skills and materials.

If political and emotional blocks are removed, the situation can become fairly straightforward. A certain level of quality and quantity are necessary to support services. Either an area has them or it does not. If it does, this is the end of the problem. If it does not, they must be developed or acquired through import. It may prove necessary to permit extraordinary importation of startup supplies of materials and skilled labor, at least for an interim period.

Example: to support a growing tourism industry, an area may need specialized equipment and technicians in such areas as telephone installation, kitchenware, washing machines, vacuum cleaners, and so on. If an area does not now have industries to manufacture and service such devices as automatic laundry equipment or dishwashers, it may be necessary to issue special import permits covering startup supplies and to permit a cadre of managers and technicians to live temporarily in the area to start an industry.

At this point in the market study, the important thing is to recognize that there will be such requirements, to identify them, and to project alternatives for developmental or corrective measures.

Land Availability

On the surface, this requirement seems deceptively simple: if you are going to build a tourism industry, you have to have enough land, in suitable locations, for the necessary facilities. Selection and evaluation of land require special expertise and care. For example, the authors have looked at a number of potential tourist service facilities in southern California and found them unsuitable because of wind, rain, or smog conditions.

In surveying available land resources, it must be recognized that tourism is a highly synergistic endeavor. There must be ready access to sources of labor, to vendors, and to communication and interchange between related functions. If accessibility and convenience for all of these factors are not present, tourism success — at least on a large scale — becomes highly improbable.

Labor Force

Tourism can truthfully be called a highly labor-intensive undertaking. This, in many areas, is one of its great attractions. A successful tourism program creates jobs. Further, the jobs created are highly attractive in many labor markets: tourism uses large quantities of unskilled and semi-skilled personnel. Therefore, tourism can fit in ideally for an area with high unemployment among unsophisticated residents.

Thus, during the early phases of a tourism study, it is important to ascertain that there is a sufficient supply of labor available. Having done this, it then becomes essential to make sure that the area selected for tourism development provides adequate living quarters for the projected labor force.

This can be a substantial problem. Consider: tourism facilities represent a relatively high standard of living. The labor force needed to support a tourism facility, however, will require substantial amounts of low and moderate-priced housing. Is this available or potentially available? If it is necessary to create low-cost housing in a tourism area, will it have a downgrading effect on the whole area?

A requirement mentioned previously in the discussion of support industries may also be present in providing labor for actual operation of tourism and accommodation facilities. That is, it may be necessary to waive immigration restrictions temporarily to bring in a cadre of technicians and management personnel to initiate or expand tourism facilities. However, at least on the technical end of things, any area with a labor supply of persons with sound attitudes can expect to train the personnel it needs within a short time. The only exception may be experienced, long-term management personnel. It may be necessary for some time to recruit qualified facilities managers in the international marketplace.

Note the comment about importance of attitudes in personnel development. Living quarters and proximity to tourist facilities have a bearing on attitude; but there is much more which comprises the composite attitude of a labor force. People have to like what they are doing and to do it willingly. If people feel and act exploited, tourism success will suffer. Thus, a constructive attitude ranks with available supply and housing facilities as a prerequisite for meeting labor requirements for a developing or a growing tourism industry.

Capital Availability

Tourism tends to cast an attractive image as an investment opportunity. For public-sector sources of capital, the stimulation of the entire economy which comes with the recycling of tourist dollars holds great appeal. Tourism makes jobs. And jobs are good politics.

For private-sector investors, tourist-related ventures have attractions through a high level of security and good prospects for appreciation in a rising economy. The security of tourism investments stems from the fact that tourism development is, in a sense, land banking. Throughout the civilized world, land values promise to appreciate strongly and continuously. There is a motto among a segment of the investment community which holds that there is only so much land, that no more can be manufactured. For investors with this outlook, land ownership represents primary security.

Further, tourism investments show strong patterns of appreciation in inflationary times. Consider a hotel. A large initial investment is required. However, the property is typically secured by a substantial mortgage repaid from earnings. The interest rate and the monetary values for this mortgage are fixed at the time of investment. But the rates charged for accommodations in the hotel will be highly responsive to inflationary trends. Thus, room rates can be expected to rise in coordination with the general economic spiral. It is accepted that hotels will maintain a fixed percentage of profit in proportion to overall sales. This consistency of profit percentage means that debt servicing expenses, which remain fixed, become a proportionately smaller segment of revenues. Thus, in an inflationary market, cash flow increases with economic trends.

Typically, therefore, the banking community in any given area will tend to welcome tourism development — providing initial research proves that prospects are soundly based. This does not mean, however, that tourism investments will routinely be oversubscribed. The money has to be there first. Thus, the survey of capital availability should include preliminary understandings and commitments from sources of investment capital, both within and external to the area.

Governmental Attitudes

Tourism, like any other segment of an economy, operates on a principle of give and take. However, governmental organizations which control tourism frequently unbalance the give/take equation. It is normal to expect a return. If expectations degenerate, prospects suffer unavoidably.

The importance of governmental attitudes cannot be underestimated. Government sets the economic climate in which tourism exists, prospers, or declines. In evaluating these attitudes, a certain amount of subjectivity is necessary. Persons performing the survey must decide, quite frankly, whether government position statements represent lip service or commitment. Further, it must be determined whether those uttering commitments have the power to back them or whether persons at higher levels in government can nullify expectations and commitments at will.

Part of this evaluation lies in appraising the nationalistic attitude prevalent in the country or area at the time. During emotional nationalistic outbreaks, the balance of international economic give and take suffers. Investments from outside sources become unattractive. Even internal investors are apt to hesitate for fear that the industry they build will be suddenly and arbitrarily nationalized. Obviously, objectivity and impartiality are essential in performing this evaluation.

PROJECTING THE POTENTIAL

All of the foregoing study areas involve the collecting of data and the formulation of conclusions and recommendations about how each factor contributes to existing tourism volumes and how it could contribute if a decision is made to expand tourism in the area. At the conclusion of this preliminary market survey, findings and analyses are incorporated in a report which, typically, is entitled *"Forecast of Visitor Volumes."*

This report is, in effect, a forecast of tourism impact and income on the basis of a number of factors and assumptions. It is designed specifically to serve as a basis for the critical decision on whether to proceed with the rest of the studies and plans which will develop the conceptual plan. Specific content of the forecast and the report in which it is incorporated should include:

1. Historical volumes and growth patterns for the local tourism industry should be traced to the extent possible, in total and according to major markets.

2. Comparative data on competing tourism areas — those which offer similar attractions and attempt to serve the same general markets — should be presented and analyzed.

3. A base year for tourism projections must be established. Typically, this will be the first year for which comprehensive data are available.

4. From the base year, the forecasts should show projected growth rates. They should indicate short-range, medium-range and long-range expectations based on several factors:

   a. Anticipated growth rates should be extrapolated on the basis of historical patterns. That is, assuming that nothing is done to build tourism in the area, these figures would show what could be expected if historical trends continue.

   b. Historical trends and projections indicating competitive market share for the local area should be shown. This is, in effect, an extrapolation aimed at showing the competitive position of the local area. Again, this projection is based on a straightforward extrapolation of historical data.

   c. Projections are made on the basis of assumed changes in the local tourism industry. Factors considered here are projected changes in transportation, facilities, promotional efforts, organization, and service levels. In other words, should the local area go into varying levels of effort to expand its tourism, this section of the forecast shows what can be expected. Obviously, this section should also state the assumptions used for support levels and projected results. These assumptions should be presented in terms of either ranges or anticipated reliability of the projected rates of growth.

All of these projections should be stated in terms of actual, experience figures and forecasts covering numbers of visitors, lengths of stay, and spending volumes.

A market forecast is the concluding document and activity for the fourth phase of the structured tourism planning process. The survey described in this chapter is aimed at reporting on where the tourism industry for the area stands currently and determining whether market potential could support further growth. If prospects for growth seem promising, the planning process moves ahead to the remainder of the conceptual planning phase, to be reviewed in the next chapter.

SYNOPSIS

As a first step toward preparation of a conceptual plan for tourism development, a market study and resources analysis should be performed by the consulting team, in close cooperation with local officials. The market study begins with a determination of the type of tourism business which exists and can be expected. Broadly, tourism resorts or areas build upon two categories of business. They are either *destinations* or *stopovers*. A destination, in general, is a resort or area with activities and facilities which justify a tourist's stay for a week or more. It is possible to have primary and secondary destinations within established travel patterns. A stopover is a facility or area used primarily as a resting place or transit point between origin and destination or between two destinations. Tourist stays at stopovers are of short duration. Given this general identification for an area, it is necessary, next, to gather detailed statistics on the anticipated tourism market and on a profile of visitors to the area. Concurrently, the study develops a profile of the tourism experience which the area offers. This is used to match the prospects of the area with its market and growth potential. In analyzing this picture, a checklist of resources to be evaluated is provided. Categories on this checklist include: cultural/historical, environmental, recreational, entertainment, shopping and dining, architecture, transportation, support industries, land, labor force, capital, and governmental attitudes. The first seven of these resource categories constitute the image which an area or resort projects in the marketplace. The rest are operational, or functional, necessities for tourism success.

REVIEW QUESTIONS

1. Describe the basic categories into which a tourism resort or area can fit.

2. For your area or one with which you are familiar, describe which category applies and why.

3. Describe the differences and relationships between environmental, recreational, and entertainment resources for a tourism resort or area.

4. For your area or one with which you are familiar, describe the strengths and weaknesses of available resources in the same categories: environmental, recreational, and entertainment.

5. For your area or one with which you are familiar, describe strengths and weaknesses of the available labor force as a resource for tourism development. In doing this, consider the factors of housing, transportation, education, and training.

6

CONCEPTUAL PLANNING

GETTING DOWN TO ACTUAL PLANNING

Although the development of a market survey like the one described in the previous chapter is, broadly, part of the conceptual planning phase of a tourism study, that activity is actually preparatory in nature. The market survey, if conducted effectively, outlines prospects in terms of anticipated tourism volumes and revenues. If the market survey is sufficiently encouraging, work will proceed for preparation of a conceptual plan.

Assuming the potential exists, the conceptual plan involves a series of studies and decisions aimed at determining what the resort or area should be in a tourism sense and how it should get there.

In general, conceptual planning will be undertaken by the same people who perform the market survey, with land-use specialists and engineers added to the group. Many of the steps or activities described here as part of conceptual planning are actually performed in parallel or in direct conjunction with the market survey. Where this happens, the planning steps, in their formal sense, become a matter of committing findings or decisions to paper and formalizing them to the extent necessary to secure a commitment to proceed further.

CONCEPTUAL PLANNING PROCESS

The steps in conceptual planning, once the market survey has been performed, include:

- Statements of objectives and policies. The planning team indicates its concept of what the tourism industry in this area should look like in terms of such elements as theme, strengths upon which the tourism industry is to be built, constraints, targeted volumes, and financial returns.
- Site selection.
- Facilities requirements.
- Supplementary attractions.
- Land-use allocation and control.
- Architectural styles and themes.
- Budgets.
- Government policies and legislative requirements.

Steps in this planning process are discussed in the remainder of this chapter.

STATEMENTS OF OBJECTIVES AND POLICIES

Statements of objectives incorporated in conceptual plans remain within the framework of but are more specific and detailed than those framed as part of the preliminary position statement (described in Chapter 4). The statements developed as part of conceptual planning provide a framework for all of the studies, plans, and recommendations which will follow. In performing the market survey which preceded this step, the idea was to be as broad and general as possible. Once the formal statements of objectives and policies have been accepted, however, the activities which follow use these boundaries. The objectives and policies set the tone and framework for the scope and content of everything which follows.

The statements, in turn, are based upon the resources studied and the assumptions made in the course of the market survey about status and potential for the tourism industry in the area. In effect, the statements of objectives and policies represent evaluations and conclusions developed subjectively on the basis of the market analysis.

Statements of objectives and policies generally temper or modify the stated potential of a market survey. Some businessmen will call this a margin of safety. Others will call it conservative practice. The point is that very few experienced businessmen will set out in a new or growing venture to achieve maximum identified potential. Thus, if a market survey indicates that an area can increase its tourism revenues fivefold, it will not be unusual to have statements of objectives aimed at doubling or tripling revenues. Very few areas will go for the maximum.

Within a conceptual plan, objectives and policies are frequently stated according to subject groups or categories. One typical breakdown, used in the presentation which follows, includes objectives and policies in these categories:

- Economic/financial
- Image or character
- Targets and strengths
- Constraints.

Economic/Financial

It is also typical that the framing of statements of objectives and policies will begin with consideration of projected volumes and financial returns. This is done even though the economic objectives are frequently carried at the end of formal statements of objectives. The fact remains that all other considerations in objective setting lead up to targeted economic results.

Having determined where decision makers want the area to go economically, the researchers proceed to frame supporting statements which provide guidelines for utilizing identified resources to achieve the targeted economic goals.

Image or Character

Consideration of the theme or motif to be followed in tourism development generally comes after establishment of economic objectives. This is a matter of considering and deciding which resources or attractions will bring in the target volume of tourism. This should be done selectively if possible. That is, if an area has only one potential theme or attraction, there may be no choice. The only decisions open will be the extent to which available resources will be utilized. However, if a range of resources and opportunities for attractions is available, the way objectives and policies are framed will go a long way toward deciding what the area will look like in the future.

For example, New York City has subsisted as a tourism attraction on the intensive activities offered in the area. In so doing, the city and its environs have actually permitted many beaches and other types of resources to deteriorate. Similarly, Las Vegas has built its tourism industry on casino gaming and glittering night life. In so doing, the area has bypassed potential attractions with western and desert themes. By comparison, Palm Springs, California, attracts many of the same people who visit Las Vegas by using a theme of quiet relaxation and leisurely sports, such as golf and tennis. It could be said that Las Vegas and Palm Springs have followed opposite themes, each building tourism industries which have met the objectives of respective decision makers.

Targets and Strengths

Statements of objectives and policies should indicate the kinds of tourists an area wants to attract and the resources to be allocated for this purpose. This serves to set priorities and establish operating guidelines. Objectives covering image or character serve to determine the type of tourists to be attracted and the markets from which they will come. Nonetheless, it is best to include formal identification of types of tourists to which an area will cater and their originating markets. Along with this, there should be statements covering the strengths which an area is expected to display in the selected marketplace. Strengths should be stated in terms of resources to be committed and/or utilized.

Constraints

Following identification of strengths, there should also be specific and clear descriptions of any constraints which apply to tourism development. This can be highly important. There may be resources in the area — in most areas there are some — which decision makers do not wish to commit to tourism development. There may, for example, be residential areas which planners do not wish to commercialize. There may be cultural traits which planners feel are unsuitable or undesirable to expose to tourists. There may be resources which may be simply too expensive to develop, such as a remote ski area which, to be popularized, would require major road building, sewage facilities, lifts, and other infrastructure support. Or there may be resources which planners wish to hold in a kind of reserve for future tourism development but do not wish to commit within the scope of the present planning activity. If these constraints are not stated, people involved in tourism development will have no way of knowing what they are or that they are to be respected.

Scope

Although statements of objectives and policies are summaries, they should be complete enough to cover the full scope of the area's tourism industry and the resources which will be committed to its development and/or expansion. Thus, statements of objectives and policies developed during conceptual planning can be rather extensive.

SITE SELECTION

At the conceptual planning level, site selection consists chiefly of locating the gateways, staging areas, resorts, destinations, attractions, and facilities which will be needed to support the new or expanding tourism program. This activity also involves relating the key sites to each other, and to certain prerequisites for their future existence. These prerequisites include:

- Accessibility
- Traffic patterns
- View
- Exposure to natural elements
- Labor supply availability.

In most instances, site selection in conceptual planning will be aimed at locating the tourism areas and facilities in broad geographic terms rather than trying to establish specific boundaries. The site allocations should follow the pattern of utilization needed to support the logical, anticipated activities of visitors. These follow predictable patterns which begin at arrival, or gateway, sites. From there, the visitation pattern proceeds through staging, to a destination (which may be selected from two or more available sites) to attractions or activities, and back through a gateway (which may be different from the entry point) for departure. Sites for all of these functions should be identified in a conceptual plan.

Figure 6-1 is a map showing selection of sites for tourism use. This illustrates the level of detail appropriate for a conceptual plan.

FACILITIES REQUIREMENTS

Based on volumes of tourism forecast and the theme selected as part of the statements of objectives and policies, it is necessary, in a separate activity, to plan at a conceptual level for the facilities which will be needed to support and serve visitors. An important input to this activity is the review of existing facilities and capabilities incorporated in the market study. In effect, the idea is to compare existing capabilities with future demands and plan for differences. Areas rating specific attention include facilities for transportation operations, lodging, feeding, support for recreational activities, and entertainment. Planning goes to a level of general definition of requirements and broad location guidelines. Specific design of facilities, a far more costly process, takes place during master planning.

SUPPLEMENTARY ATTRACTIONS

The theme selected and the resources allocated to support it constitute the main, or primary, attraction for bringing people into an area. Once these are established, it can be extremely profitable to provide supplementary attractions giving visitors additional things to do. From the standpoint of tourism development management, the logic is straightforward: if visitors stay longer, the entire economy will benefit from the extended utilization of lodging, feeding, services, and other establishments.

For each supplementary attraction, it is a sound practice to think of holding the attention of visitors for anywhere from a half day to one full day. For planning purposes, it is usually wise to tie attraction development to the cultural or natural attributes of the area. Further, there should be enough traffic anticipated to support the attraction financially.

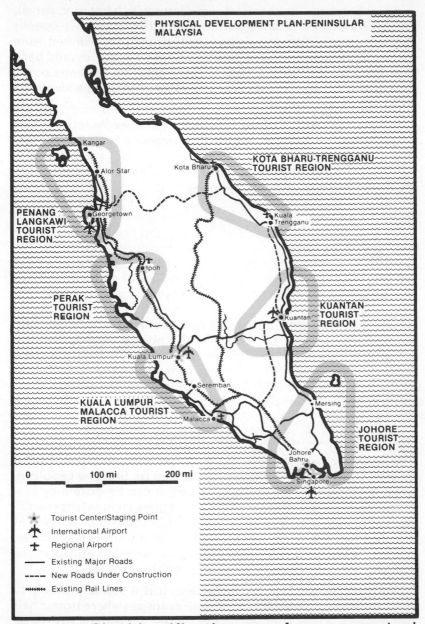

Figure 6-1. Site-identification map from conceptual plan for tourism development.

Example: the Polynesian Cultural Center on the island of Oahu has proven an excellent supplementary attraction for the Hawaiian tourism industry. Many thousands of tourists spend a full day traveling to and visiting this center. The facility itself is easily self-supporting. It represents an activity which fills out a visit for people who might otherwise become bored. The volume of tourism in Hawaii is ideal for support of such a facility.

Similarly, Mexico City has constructed museums for archeology and modern art in proximity to each other within Chapultepec Park. Large numbers of visitors pay admission fees which help support these important cultural centers. These facilities themselves have become highlights in either extending or filling out tourism visits to Mexico City.

During conceptual planning, the idea is to identify opportunities for this type of supplementary attraction and to draw broad guidelines for their development, including location preferences.

LAND-USE ALLOCATION AND CONTROL

During conceptual planning, zoning considerations are important. The activity does not move to the level of detail which involves specific parcels of land. Rather, concentration is on conditions and types of use. The idea is to use land appropriately, deriving maximum benefits from natural resources and existing development while establishing economic guidelines for using available areas. To illustrate, it would not make sense to zone beach front land for a small number of private houses while hotels were placed inland. At the same time, it would also not make sense to develop beach front land to such density (as many resorts have done) that the leisurely pace and roominess of a sunshine resort was destroyed.

Considerations taken into account in promulgating broad zoning specifications should include:

- Open areas or green belts
- Residential areas
- Commercial areas by type and density (three or four grades of commercial or manufacturing properties)
- Density of commercial development
- Building-to-site-size ratios of land utilization
- Restrictions covering floor space for size of land

- Construction height restrictions
- Setback restrictions
- Consideration of landmarks or other special terrain features.

Overall, the zoning objectives of planners will be to establish guidelines which assure a balance between aesthetics, terrain, and commercial realties. Land-use planners have to bear in mind that they cannot constrain or restrict land use to a level where the area becomes unattractive to private-sector investors. At the same time, they cannot permit overdevelopment to an extent where the area will be forced into a rapid decline. The job of the planners at this stage, in general, is to balance land utilization in the area with the local economy, the future impact of tourism, and the best interests of long-range profitability.

ARCHITECTURAL STYLES AND THEMES

Unity in architectural style and appearance, particularly when patterned upon the traditions and culture of the area, can be an asset in building the image of the area in the minds of prospective tourists. For example, tourism areas in Tahiti use a *fare* (thatched roof) appearance. In Taxco, all architecture follows a Mexican Colonial theme. In San Francisco and New York, emphasis is on high-rise buildings with views of wide areas of the city.

Over and above the value of architectural themes in presenting a pleasing aspect to tourists, architecture also plays an important role in the acceptance of tourism facilities by local residents. Architecture which jars or offends local residents can have an extremely negative effect on tourism development.

At the conceptual planning level, this activity can be relatively brief, concentrating upon a general statement and illustrations covering theme and style.

BUDGETS

Some financial projection is necessary to put all of the other functional elements of a conceptual plan into perspective. Since other aspects of the plan are stated as generalities, financial projections at this point cannot be much more than approximations. Budgets associated with conceptual plans are sometimes presented as "order-of-magnitude" estimates.

Because this element of a conceptual plan is so tenuous, it is important to include descriptions of the bases and/or assumptions used for estimates. At this point, emphasis within financial projections should be on costs. By nature, tourism development requires heavy front-end commitments of capital before appreciable cash flow begins. In a conceptual plan, this characteristic should be presented clearly. Income projections should then reflect this perspective.

Budgets should not be either understated or overly optimistic. People using conceptual plans can regard approximated budgets literally. There will frequently be attempts to make the actual develoment specifications prepared later conform to estimated budgets prepared without benefit of design detailing. Therefore, preliminary budgets are not the place for optimism or understatement.

GOVERNMENT POLICES AND LEGISLATIVE REQUIREMENTS

This portion of the conceptual plan builds upon the study of governmental attitudes incorporated in the market survey. The market survey analyzes and reports on government attitudes, policies, and positions as they exist and as they relate to tourism. These findings are analyzed in the light of objectives for the tourism industry and as changes or requirements for new legislation or policies are described.

At this point, planners should develop specific lists for policies and legislation which will be needed in such areas as investment codes, tax codes, customs and import duties, immigration policies, and government organization requirements for support of the increased tourism activity. In effect, these recommendations tell decision makers what must be done by government entities to place the area in a competitive position to attract visitors and investors. In developing these recommendations, similar codes from competitive countries or areas should be referenced.

IDENTIFYING AND DEALING WITH WEAKNESSES

Of necessity, the main thrust of a market analysis and projection will lie in identifying strengths of an area, attraction, or resort and assessing their prospective value in terms of tourism visits and revenues. This optimism can color inputs to conceptual planning.

In evaluating market prospects, planners should, at some point, simulate (or think through) the potential tourist's experience to identify weaknesses or shortcomings in the resort or area. Most often, this process is undertaken in terms of infrastructure or support requirements. Planners call upon engineers and qualified technicians to identify needs for roads, parking, transportation, feeding, and sanitation facilities. These are all obvious necessities.

It is valuable also to look at a tourist's exposure and experience subjectively. For example, if an area's strengths can be classified as daytime activities, there may not be enough evening entertainment to occupy visitors. Or, if cultural attractions predominate, there may be a shortage of multilingual guides and printed materials.

In general, planners are well advised to look at and find fault with the rosy picture which tends to be developed in identifying and evaluating positive attractions or features. The sooner the negative forces are identified, evaluated, and resolved, the better will be the results of any development program, of any magnitude.

As conceptual planning proceeds, findings and recommendations on all of these topics should be committed to writing and incorporated in a formal report. Also included in this report should be a management summary, including a timetable, which incorporates recommendations on the key decisions which should be made and the commitments to be undertaken. The report of the conceptual planning activity, then, becomes the basis for the management decision on whether to proceed with master planning, to proceed with partial implementation of the proposed program, to modify or alter the direction of tourism development, or to abort the tourism-planning effort altogether. Factors which bear upon this decision are covered in the next chapter. Completion of the conceptual plan concludes the fifth phase of the project structure for tourism planning.

SYNOPSIS

The market study (described in the last chapter) provides the basis for conceptual planning. The conceptual plan, in effect, describes the resort or tourism area to be developed to realize the potential identified in the market study. The steps followed in conceptual planning, each of which will generally become a section of the plan itself, include:

- Statements of objectives and policies
- Site Selection
- Facilities requirements
- Supplementary attractions
- Land-use allocation and control
- Architectural styles and themes
- Budgets
- Government policies and legislative requirements.

All work and documentation are carried out at a general, or overview, level. For example, potential sites for accommodations and facilities are related to areas where they should logically be located. But the work is not detailed to the level of exact geographic boundaries or engineering specifications. In composite, the conceptual plan provides a general view of the future tourism development program and the steps necessary to achieve targeted results.

REVIEW QUESTIONS

1. Describe the reasons for and differences between statements of objectives which are incorporated in a preliminary position statement and in a conceptual plan.

2. For your area or one with which you are familiar, draft a set of statements of objectives and policies describing constraints which should be applied to tourism development.

3. Describe the differences and relationships between sites used for gateways, staging, destination areas or resorts, and supporting attractions.

4. Describe, from the visitor's viewpoint, the flow and relationship of events in a typical vacation in your area or one with which you are familiar.

5. Describe the value of a unified architectural style or theme in tourism development of an area.

6. Comment upon or criticize the functional and aesthetic integration impacting the tourist's experience in your area or one with which you are familiar.

7

DECISION
TIME

SIGNIFICANCE

All study efforts, no matter how interesting they may be and how much attention they generate, should come to an end sooner or later. Conceptual planning and the broad-gauge studies it involves will go on for varying lengths of time in different areas. Generally, the very fact that tourism is being studied with professional assistance will uncover a number of facets which tend to extend the areas covered and time consumed by market studies and conceptual plans.

Part of the decision maker's responsibility, however, lies in holding some kind of rein on the conceptual planning process. The idea is to bring the study efforts to an appropriate conclusion at a logical time. When this happens, the decision makers should have:

- An overview on the historic development and potential opportunities for tourism in the area

- Data on a series of alternative steps which can be taken in building or expanding tourism
- A recommended plan of action for tourism development.

Now the responsibility shifts. The decision maker has probably not taken an active role in day-to-day performance of the market survey and conceptual planning. Now it can be said that the ball has been bounced into the court of the decision maker. It is up to the decision makers to take the steps and commit the actions necessary to move the effort into its next phase — or to alter or terminate the project. It is, in short, decision time.

Simply recognizing that there is a formal, critical decision to be made is an important step in management of the tourism-development process. In all too many areas, there has been a tendency simply to let tourism development be carried on a tide of enthusiasm and decision-by-default. A decision-making void creates an environment in which planners simply continue their efforts, permitting decisions to be made on a *de facto* basis, without benefit of formal commitment or approved plan.

The first significance of this phase in the tourism-development process, then, lies in the very fact of its existence. This represents recognition that the enterprise is at a critical juncture where business judgment must be applied and a businessman's commitment must be made. Up to this point, planning and survey activities, for all their breadth, have not had a discernible physical impact on the area or property. Few people have been affected. No land has been condemned or acquired. Nothing significant has been changed.

The next step, however, is a big one. For one thing, a decision to go ahead with master planning will call for a commitment of funds in the order of five to 10 times greater than those expended to date.

Perhaps an even greater impact will occur in social and political areas. Master planning involves such activities as the delineation of specific sites, the design of facilities, the assembly of parcels of land, and the complexities of writing, introducing, and passing enabling legislation.

The significance of the decision to proceed with master planning, then, centers around the increased scale and scope of commitments to be made and the changes they will initiate.

EXPOSURE

Also impacting the importance of a formal decision at this point is the fact that the tourism program will be "going public" in the truest sense of this term. Once such activities as land acquisition and legislative planning get into full swing, the tourism program will become a matter of public knowledge and public attention. Invariably, when changes affecting culture and lifestyle are at stake, disagreement of some sort will ensue. Accusations will inevitably be made. The people who have authorized the activities which will come under criticism or active fire had better be aware that these things will happen. They had better be ready to explain their decisions, possibly to defend them.

In short, a decision to go ahead with master planning for a tourism industry may become a time for choosing sides. The persons responsible for the decision to proceed will have to be committed to their decisions if they are to succeed. These decisions will lead inevitably to change. Change often begets unrest. But change is also essential to progress. Successful change, in turn, depends upon the diligence and skill which go into planning and preparation.

THE DECISION PROCESS

One of the necessary ingredients for an effective decision is a professional approach, or process, for weighing alternatives and reaching a conclusion. Specifically, the decision makers should recognize and guide themselves toward a decision which is based on acceptance, rejection, or modification of specific recommendations which result from conceptual planning. Thus, at the outset, the decision makers should be sure that they have viable, understandable decision alternatives. They should understand what these alternatives are and be clear on the consequences of selection of any of the options open to them.

To illustrate, suppose an area currently functioning as a secondary destination has an airport with 5,200-foot runways capable of handling short-range jets only. Suppose a conceptual plan calls for lengthening runway capacity to 10,000 feet and building terminal facilities for jumbo jets. Projections show a 10-year recovery of investments through property and use taxes, as well as from proceeds stemming from a doubling of visitor volumes and a 125 percent growth in direct revenues. Alternatives outlined for consideration and selection might include:

- The full plan for runways and terminal facilities could be approved.

- There could be staged implementation, possibly with makeshift terminal arrangements initially to be replaced only after cash flow from business increases has been realized.

- The airport could be left as it is and air shuttle service to the nearest jumbo-jet facility increased, perhaps through subsidies.

- One always-available alternative is to do nothing.

These are, of course, simplifications of complex situations. These examples do, however, illustrate the principle that it is possible to delineate a specific set of choices for decision selection. For each choice, probable consequences should be described to a level which permits objective evaluation.

The thing which should *not* occur at this point is a deterioration of the decision-making process into a debating session. In general, this should not be a time for introducing or considering new alternatives. This is not to say that new alternatives may not be desirable. Rather, it is important that managers recognize the nature of the decision-making process in which they are involved. At this point, the alternatives for future directions in the tourism industry should have been identified, explored, and evaluated. The decision makers should be acting upon recommendations or choosing between alternatives which have been presented clearly to them.

If the decision-making deliberations uncover additional alternatives which have not previously been considered, it is possible that something was wrong in conceptual planning. At very least, the decision makers themselves should not become embroiled in launching new studies. If a new alternative appears attractive enough to warrant consideration, it should be studied and evaluated separately from the decision-making process, which must remain objective if it is to be effective.

DECISION SCOPE

A well-drawn conceptual plan for tourism development will be modular. That is, there should be an overall recommendation for adoption and action, as well as a series of separate parts which can be isolated and implemented independently. In general, it would be poor strategy to present a single set of decision alternatives on a take-it-or-leave-it basis. Such a course of action would represent either arrogance or foolhardiness (or both) on the part of the researchers and planners. In the real world, developmental decisions on tourism industries are usually made by political groups of mixed membership. At very best, the commitments and decisions reached by such groups can be expected to represent some measure of compromise. To abet the process of compromise, modularity in program segments and alternatives is a virtual necessity.

It is important, then, that decision makers understand what they are being asked to commit to and that recommendations offered to them be designed on a modular basis. It should be considered necessary that recommendations for development and implementation of a tourism program follow a realistic philosophy which recognizes that half a loaf can be a lot better than nothing at all. Decision makers, too, should be able to apply the resources at their command — or which they are willing to commit — according to their own priorities. The proposals considered should facilitate decision making which favors implementing components of plans on a modular basis.

DECISION STATEMENT

Just as decision makers should expect those reporting to them to consider their situation, so also should decisions reached be stated clearly and specifically. When decision makers determine what they want done, they should state this clearly, in both verbal and financial terms. That is, the decision makers should issue statements indicating what they expect to accomplish and how much they expect to spend. These descriptions should be written and delivered to everyone with a stake in the project.

END PRODUCT

Typically, the end product of this decision-making process will be a request for proposal (RFP) — or a group of RFPs — covering the master planning phase of the project. The purpose of an RFP is to provide a uniform document which can be sent to prospective consultants, architects, engineers, and other potential vendors who might be interested in proposing, or bidding, on all or a portion of the work involved in master planning.

The development of RFP documents for tourism studies was described and illustrated in Chapter 4. The same principles can be applied at this point.

The issuing of the RFP or group of RFPs represents an implementation of decision-making responsibilities for persons who control use of land suitable for tourism development. The distribution of RFPs to prospective vendors underscores the commitment which has been made.

In discussing master planning, the chapters which follow cover this massive phase in a tourism-development project according to the major specialties or disciplines involved.

SYNOPSIS

Within the structure recommended for a tourism project, the decision discussed in this chapter is the first of two phases established specifically for decision making. This project organization provides the discipline to help assure that persons responsible for conceptual planning state recommendations and decision alternatives clearly — and that decision makers state their commitments clearly. A condition to be avoided is the degeneration of the decision process into a series of debates and arguments over identification of new possibilities or alternatives. If new opportunities are uncovered, they should be studied and presented in activities separate from the decision-making process.

REVIEW QUESTIONS

1. Describe the purposes of separating decision making from activities involving planning and research for tourism development.

2. Describe some problems which could be encountered if activities for planning and decision making were carried out together, by the same people.

3. Explain why it is useful to frame recommendations from conceptual planning in modules for separate consideration of a variety of alternatives.

8

THE
MASTER
PLAN

SCOPE

Master planning is an activity which involves working with and for the development of the approved portions of the conceptual plan. As discussed in the last chapter, an effective way to structure a conceptual plan is to establish a series of modules, providing decision alternatives for each. This means that, in acting upon a conceptual plan, the decision makers can apply judgment to the selection of parts of a tourism program they wish to implement and also to the degree to which they want to proceed.

The continuing tourism-development program will then be a composite of selected modules. The coordination and integration of these modules, along with the detailing of their design and scheduling of necessary work, establish the boundaries, or scope, of master planning. Putting it another way, the selected, approved portions of the conceptual plan become the framework within which master planning takes place.

PLANNING LEVEL

Master planning is carried out at a far greater depth of technical and design detail than conceptual planning. One way to illustrate the greater extent of the work involved is through the time and money which are typically involved. As indicated earlier, it is not at all unusual to find situations in which commitments for time and money expended in master planning are 10 *times* as great as they are for conceptual planning.

Differences in the type of work and amount of effort involved between conceptual and master planning can be illustrated with the example of a relationship between an architect and client who has commissioned the design and building of a home. The home-building project is usually carried through in a series of stages. Initially, the architect and client confer to establish general objectives about size, styling, and features of the home. The understanding which comes from this conference is much like that which emerges from a preliminary study of tourism potential. At this point, the architect will probably prepare some rough pencil sketches as a basis for discussion and preliminary agreement.

Based on the understanding developed at this point, the architect can give the client a general description of what the home will look like and what it would cost to proceed with the next step in design. This step will probably call for preliminary diagrams showing how the house will fit onto the owner's parcel of land. Also included will be a more formal sketch or drawing of the house. This sketch is frequently executed in color and mounted for presentation and display. A drawing of this type is known as an architect's rendering. In terms of the tourism project structure, this rendering corresponds with the work which tourism planners can expect to have completed at the conclusion of the conceptual planning phase of the project.

Once a commitment is reached upon the architect's rendering and preliminary plans for a home, detailed planning of landscape features and building structures takes place. The same, generally, is true in tourism development: approval of specific modules and options within a conceptual plan leads to a deeper level and greater extent of planning, resulting in a master plan.

Where a conceptual plan, for example, might indicate a necessity to increase capacity of airport runways and terminal facilities, the master plan would go on to indicate the specific land to be used, the configuration of the runways, and the structural appearance and layouts for the enhanced terminals. Similarly, where a conceptual plan might indicate a general area, such as a beach and its environs, to be set aside for resort and hotel development, the master plan would go into specifics about site location of facilities, complete with specifications on how land areas will be developed. Architectural renderings for the buildings would also be provided.

There are differences, of course, between the planning of the home by an architect and master planning of an attraction or major tourism destination. One major difference is that the architect dealing with owners of moderate-sized pieces of property can proceed with details and specifics which go beyond the authorization limits of most master planners. Master planners operating on behalf of the public sector, for example, would specifically not be empowered to execute detailed plans for facilities to be built and operated by private-sector entities. To illustrate, a public-sector planner could identify and specify a site for a resort or hotel. A general conceptual presentation of the location and appearance of the accommodations and recreation facilities could be provided by the public sector. But understandably, it would be undesirable to spend public-sector funds to go into detailed engineering-type plans covering water supply, drainage, roadways, and engineering details for structures. These are responsibilities — and expenses — which should be undertaken by the ultimate owners and operators of the facilities.

A master plan, however, does include projected developmental budgets for both public and private-sector investments, as well as projected income and expense statements carried forward at least to the point of projected profitability, usually five years or more.

MASTER PLANNING SKILLS

Because of the broad scope and projected impact of tourism development upon a destination, master planning is, invariably a team effort. A broad range of disciplines and skills must be involved. The major specialties required, the responsibilities, and results expected, are described in subsequent chapters of this book. For the purposes of this overview, however, the master planning effort can be seen as divided into two broad categories:

1. Operational/Services
2. Technical/Facilities.

In general, the first category — operational/services — will require consultants and staff with people-oriented dispositions and skills. These will be the experienced financial and managerial consultants, hotel managers, restaurateurs, transportation managers, and others whose strengths lie in serving the people. The second group will be made up of professionals and technicians who tend to be engineering and construction oriented — architects, civil engineers, environmental technologists, and land-utilization specialists.

In general also, these separate groups will work in sequence as well as in coordination with each other. That is, operational planning must come first in a majority of cases. Then technicians enter the picture *to plan for the facilities to meet operational needs.* A coordination effort takes place during which technical plans are defined and modified to meet operational specifications or operational plans are modified to conform to environmental or technical constraints. Most typically, operating plans will be modified to conform to realities uncovered or presented by the technicians. This is easily illustrated.

A golf course is specified for a location which is ideal for its proximity to hotels, scenery, general land and environmental characteristics, and so on. On studying this site, technical people of varying disciplines might determine that the area is subject to flooding or to heavy winds which would make it *untenable* for use as a golf course. Obviously, operating plans are modified.

MASTER PLANNING FRAMEWORK

Most of the rest of this book will deal with key areas or requirements for operational and technical planning. Discussions center around key disciplines or functional requirements for the building or growth of a tourism industry. Within the context of this discussion on overall planning, however, it is important to recognize that there are also two distinct types of services and facilities requirements which form a framework for the master planning and implementation efforts which follow. These service-requirement areas are:

- The staging function

- Tourism activities.

THE STAGING FUNCTION

Staging is referred to as a function rather than an area, as is sometimes done, because lines of demarcation between job and geography are not always absolute. In general, staging involves the receiving and dispatching of tourists for entry from outside the area and for exit to other destinations. As part of its function, staging involves transportation, accommodation, services such as shopping and other amenities.

The importance of identifying staging as a separate function and of focusing planning attention upon it centers around the fact that a tourism industry literally stands or falls on its ability to meet staging requirements. If an area cannot receive tourists and set the stage for pleasant stays, the entire industry will suffer. Similarly, if an area cannot cap off a pleasant stay by a tourist with a happy departure, the experience will leave a bad taste which will sour prospects for the industry as a whole.

Staging is also important because the areas which perform this function are the most heavily impacted by tourism traffic and undergo the greatest degree of change. Therefore, planning and development of staging capabilities, as well as definition for the role they will play in the overall tourism program, can be critically important to continuing success.

In recent years, with increased service on airline routes, the staging function has been reduced, in most major air terminals, largely to a matter of in-transit processing. Consider Honolulu International Airport, for example. The majority of airline routes between the Pacific and the United States mainland stop at Honolulu. Inbound, United States customs and immigration clearances are performed at Honolulu. Outbound, the planes face the longest legs of their journeys and must be completely refueled and reserviced. Thus, travelers find themselves staged through Honolulu for periods ranging between one and four hours. Where connections are missed, the time period can expand accordingly. But the majority of transiting passengers never leave the airport.

A few years ago, the staging function was more extensive. It was commonplace for travelers to have to "lay over" in Honolulu awaiting flights to points like Australia, New Caledonia, Fiji, Singapore, Hong Kong, Tokyo, or Taiwan. It became a common practice for individuals staying in Hawaii for eight hours or more to use hotels and facilities in Waikiki.

With longer-range jets and increased frequency of schedules, stopovers at staging points have become less extensive. However, the staging function remains critical for the success of the tourist experience. Since the airport itself frequently becomes the staging area, it is important that facilities and procedures be adapted to make stopovers and processing functions as pleasant as possible. This can be a real challenge, since large jets can tax facilities with heavy work volumes in concentrated periods.

Failure to provide adequate staging can have serious repercussions. For example, as airline travel became predominant, Philadelphia became a major staging area for travelers to Atlantic City. Failure to establish amenities and special facilities for passengers transiting between Philadelphia and Atlantic City contributed to unhappy experiences of many travelers, and to a decline in tourism.

TOURISM ACTIVITIES

Activities are what tourists do or why they come to an area. Typically, activities or attractions are planned in terms of centers, each of which represents something to do or someplace to stay for anywhere from half a day to several weeks.

An activity center can be a museum which attracts masses of people for half-day visits. An activity center can also be a theme park like Disneyland or a luxury hotel which provides a focal point for tourism visits. Increasingly, planning and thinking are running to extensive resort towns with multiple activity centers, containing all of the required accommodations and support services. Under such a concept, for example, Orlando would be a staging area, Disney World a complete resort activity center.

This type of relationship will generally apply across the board. That is, an activity center will tend to be suburban or relatively isolated, as distinct from a staging area which must be relatively urban and cosmopolitan. Thus, where a staging area can have activity centers incorporated within it, an activity center is rarely a staging area.

The development and implementation of master plans occupies both the great majority of the resources of a tourism program and of the remainder of this book. The next 10 chapters are devoted to key, specific segments of master planning and implementation. In a sense, a master plan is a compilation of the work and end results described in these chapters. This chapter has been an introduction and overview to the process of master planning. Coverage of the actual work of master planning follows.

SYNOPSIS

Master planning is a process for completing and detailing additional work on the portions of the conceptual plan which are approved for further development. The differences between conceptual and master planning lie largely in the level of detail involved. Where conceptual planning, for example, might indicate the need to expand airport runways and terminal facilities, master planning would go into specifics on land and construction. Master planning is usually a public-sector project. Though land is set aside for private-sector development and facilities may be specified in terms of capacities and general appearance, detailed engineering and structural planning tend to be left for the private-sector organizations which will develop and/or operate the properties. Facilities which represent public sector responsibilities are, however, planned in detail. Master planning processes tend to break down into skill categories involving specialists in operations and services or in technical and facilities design. The operations and services specialists are people oriented. Their planning work centers around simulations of tourism visits. The technical and facilities specialists then design the support and structural requirements for these services. Frequently, technical and structural design activities uncover problems which require redesign of the services portion of the master plan. Separation also exists between master planning for the staging function and for tourism activities. Staging is the volume function which involves processing visitors in and out of the area. Activity centers are the areas where visitors stay and enjoy the amenities which attract them to the area.

REVIEW QUESTIONS

1. Describe the differences in scope and level between conceptual and master planning.

2. Define and describe relationships between the staging function and activities centers for a major tourism destination.

3. Define and describe the differences between master planning for operations and services and for technical requirements and facilities.

9

GOVERNMENTAL OPERATIONS AND PROGRAMS

WHO MAKES TOURISM HAPPEN?

If tourism is to happen, somebody, or some organization, has to do something. But who? What kind of organization? How much power should it have? What limitations?

These are serious questions. Answers to them become easier to find if written statements of objectives were developed during earlier phases. These objectives become the description of mission for whatever organization is formed to carry forward planning, implementation, and operation of tourism programs.

If written statements of objectives had not been drafted previously, there will never be a better opportunity. If anything is going to happen, the job had better be defined. Preparing such objectives and structuring the organization to accomplish them is an early and important part of master planning.

Suppose the tourism job has been defined through formal, written objectives. Whose job is it?

One classic problem is that responsibility for tourism does not fit comfortably into conventional governmental structures or agencies. In Washington, D.C., for example, more than 30 governmental departments or agencies have at least some responsibility for tourism in the United States. However, there is no single organization with overall responsibility or authority to deal with tourism as a single entity. Tourism has just too many aspects and involvements — finance, parks and recreation, information, transportation, law enforcement, education, and others. All of these governmental functions play essential roles.

Because of this type of breadth, it isn't feasible simply to assign tourism responsibility to an existing governmental department or agency. For one thing, no single department would encompass all of the skills and background necessary. For another, the very breadth of tourism could lead to friction within normal government structures.

In every case observed by the authors, the best approach has been to set up a separate agency, department, or commission with tourism responsibility. Whatever form the agency takes, one of its functions is invariably to act as catalyst, bringing to bear existing skills and jurisdiction to support tourism development and operations.

Therefore, this discussion assumes that some sort of governmental agency specializing in tourism will be established. But this does not end organizational decision making. It is only the beginning. The next question to be faced: what responsibilities or authority will the tourism entity have?

Possibilities for assignment and/or sharing of responsibility and authority by a tourism entity are almost infinite. In general, however, governments tend to take one of two broad approaches:

1. The tourism entity can be an advisory agency entirely.

2. The tourism entity can have line authority for direct tourism operations and coordinating responsibility for other governmental facilities or resources.

Either approach works. Each approach, however, does involve potential shortcomings and advantages. In any case, it is important to recognize that tourism support involves cooperation among many jurisdictions. Thus, no matter how an organization is structured, it will take common sense and a commitment to collaboration to make it work.

One of the practical aspects associated with assuring cooperation of multiple agencies extends directly from the purse strings. If the tourism entity has or controls elements of a government's budget, it can get things done, no matter what type of organizational structure or lines are put on paper. If the entity is put in a position of beggar, very little is likely to happen.

ORGANIZATION STRUCTURE

Given that a tourism organization of some sort is necessary, what should it look like?

The first major decision lies in determining the relationship between the tourism entity and the government. Basically, there are three choices:

1. The tourism entity can be a governmental ministry, department, or agency.

2. The tourism entity can be quasi-governmental. It can, for example, have a nucleus of governmental facilities and people, combined with an advisory commission of private-industry representatives.

3. The tourism entity can be privately operated whether or not it is supported by governmental grants. Under this option, which usually applies to an area rather than an entire nation, the tourism entity is not part of government. However, if it is to function, strong government recognition of its role and function is essential. Some government subsidy might also be provided.

An example of the first type of organization can be seen in the Australian Tourism Commission, a governmental department.

The quasi-governmental approach was taken in Fiji, where responsibility has been divided between a governmental agency and a privately funded organization.

The third type of organization structure emerges when an area is developed largely through private capital. A clear-cut example can be seen in the situation of Sun Valley, Idaho, developed initially by the Union Pacific Railroad and subsequently sold to other operators. Another type of example can be seen in the situation of Las Vegas, Nevada, represented in the tourism marketplace by a strong convention and visitor's bureau.

OPERATING SAFEGUARDS

Under any of these options, it is still essential that the authority, scope, budget, and powers of the tourism agency be defined through detailed legislation. Such powers might include the authority to administer budgets appropriated specifically for tourism development and operations, the authority to conduct research and establish a research arm for continuing market analysis, the authority to develop and implement programs needed for creation of tourism facilities and services, and many others.

In drafting and securing support for such legislation, it is important to recognize the vastness of the expenditures involved and the power they represent. It is essential, therefore, to build in assurances, checks, and balances. Specifically, because large amounts of money and public lands may be involved, there are opportunities for comparatively few people to derive improper gains or to enrich themselves through misuse or questionable use of resources. In short, it is necessary that legislative acts and the programs they establish recognize that where such a great potential for enrichment exists, there is an equally great temptation for corruption.

This potential for corruption itself is often a valid argument for the establishment of a quasi-governmental agency headed by a commission of representatives from both private and public sectors. This eliminates the possibility of a situation where a few powerful bureaucrats can misuse or misdirect the allocation of funds or other resources.

Arguments against the quasi-governmental commission form of tourism agency hold that it is too easy for such bodies to be weighted in favor of private-sector gains at public expense. This possibility definitely exists. Safeguards should be stipulated and applied scrupulously to the operation of whatever tourism entity is established.

For purposes of this discussion, consider that the point about safeguards has been made. To illustrate how all of the necessary functions are incorporated within a tourism agency, it will be assumed that a hypothetic government has decided to proceed with a quasi-governmental commission, to be called the Department of Tourism. It will be assumed further that it is set up at the federal level in an emerging nation with attractive climate and a relatively small population. A table of organization for this department is shown in Figure 9-1.

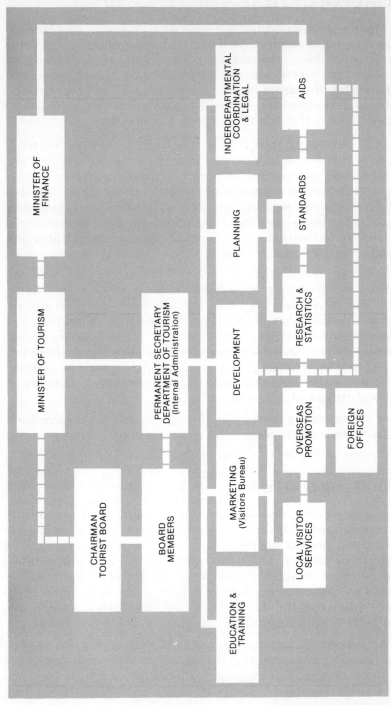

Figure 9-1. Table of organization for hypothetic department of tourism.

DEPARTMENT OF TOURISM FUNCTIONS

Broadly, the Department of Tourism is charged with planning, promoting, and administering all facets of tourism for its country. To meet these responsibilities, the organization chart recognizes certain functional requirements. Note, for example, that the minister of tourism is at cabinet level. This will make it possible for the minister to secure agreement for and assure cooperation at the highest levels of government.

This is demonstrated in Figure 9-1 by showing the minister of tourism at the same level as the minister of finance. In this case, the minister of tourism is administratively and functionally responsible for the operation of his or her department. The dotted line between the two ministers designates their conferring relationship. However, there is a solid line from the minister of finance to the division within the tourism agency which allocates and distributes funds.

Similarly, there is a dotted-line relationship between the minister and the chairman of the tourism commission for this nation. This illustrates the fact that a combined, quasi-governmental approach has been taken. The minister of tourism is a government official. The commissioners are private-sector appointees. They advise the minister but have direct responsibilities for policy setting, as illustrated by the solid-line connection between the commissioners and the permanent secretary of the Department of Tourism.

At the operating level, several functional divisions have been created and specific responsibilities have been assigned.

Marketing Division

The marketing division has both research and operational responsibilities. Operationally, the division is responsible for advertising, promotion, publicity, sales, and information services required by tourists. These responsibilities are both international and domestic in scope. Most advertising and promotional activities are aimed at markets in major tourism-origination countries. Domestically, this division provides guides, interpreters, and activity coordination for groups or individual visitors.

An economics and market research group within this division is responsible for measuring the impact of tourism development on the economy. For example, continuing research is done and data are accumulated from published sources on travel patterns, market share, effectiveness of advertising, and other information relative to the size and sources of the overall tourism market. Similarly, data on arrivals and departures accumulated by this group provide a basis for the planning of transportation, facilities, manpower, and other functions.

This group also interacts closely with the statistical bureau of the federal government. Where market information is needed, efforts are made to see if existing governmental entities can provide the required data. Independent statistical studies are commissioned only where government sources cannot fill identified needs.

Another important function of this group is to compare actual results — data on visitors and visitor activities — with projections for their area and statistics on competitive destinations. These are evaluated and reported as a basis for planning and other functions of the department of tourism.

Planning Division

The planning division is generally responsible for two separate functions:

1. Development and updating of short and long-range plans
2. Operating standards.

Most tourism authorities utilize a one-year, short-range plan which serves also as a budget projection for current operations. Most authorities also utilize a five-year plan which is updated on six-month or annual cycles. This long-range plan serves as a basis for projecting budgets, hotel-room requirements, infrastructure needs, personnel and training needs, and projections for other amenities which may be needed.

The standards section of the planning division is responsible for identifying and inventorying natural assets of the area and establishing standards for their physical development. For example, in identifying a beach area as a potential attraction, this group establishes specifications for the number and types of hotels and other facilities which can be developed according to the parameters of the nation's master plan for tourism.

The standards group also impacts the scheduling of continuing tourism development. As current activities warrant, it recommends time tables for the development of master-planned facilities awaiting such approval.

The standards group also monitors operations of existing facilities in terms of quality of service and fees. One of its responsibilities, for example, lies in keeping track of room rental rates at hotels to help guard against overcharging. The classification system established by the standards division helps with this job. Members of the staff follow criteria which identify characteristics of hotels to determine whether they can be qualified as international class, deluxe, or standard. Rate schedules within each of these classifications are kept competitive with other tourism destinations.

This standards function is a line responsibility of the department of tourism. The standards group publishes ratings which help monitor this responsibility. Publication of ratings or inspection results helps encourage hotels to maintain the caliber of facilities and services, since this group has the power to impact income of operators through reclassification.

The same group also sets licensing standards for travel agents, tour operators, and related tourist services, such as bus lines, taxicabs, and so on.

Development Division

The development division monitors actual site and construction work to be sure that planning and architectural standards are met and that tourism facilities meet the objectives and standards of the master plan. Of necessity, this group coordinates its efforts closely with architects, engineers, and operating personnel of the department of public works. The staff of this division keeps themselves posted on highway construction, maintenance, water, power, and other physical-development aspects of their country as a whole.

Education and Training Division

The education and training group is small but prestigious. It is staffed by qualified educators and educational administrators who work with the nation's vocational schools and colleges to coordinate the training of operating personnel and managers who will staff and build the tourism industry. Among the responsibilities of this group are the writing and distribution of curriculum standards. For vocational-training programs, this group issues certificates of completion for students who meet prescribed requirements at authorized schools. Working with the national university, the group is encouraging institution of a degree program in hotel and resort management. This includes the recruiting of visiting professors from other countries and the hiring of consultants to establish an appropriate curriculum.

Interdepartmental Coordination and Legal Divsion

This group specializes in knowing where the capabilities and facilities for accomplishing tourism objectives are within the government and in coordinating these resources for results. In addition, the group employs attorneys who provide legal counsel for the tourism industry.

FUNDING FOR THE TOURISM AGENCY

Obviously, the actual scope and breadth of operations established for any given department of tourism will accommodate to the pocketbook opened to them. Thus if a developing area was attempting to create a fledgling tourism industry, departments might be activated on a skeleton basis, or perhaps one at a time. (For example, the planning and development functions could be incorporated in a single unit at the outset, then split apart as workloads and the financial situation warrants.) The important thing is to establish, at the outset, how much is available, and what should be accomplished. The tourism program must then be scaled realistically to available resources. It is frequently possible to get started and then build on the basis of projected tourism revenues and departmental budgets which they generate.

The department of tourism depicted in Figure 9-1 is funded through a combination of governmental and private-sector contributions. Governmental funding is through a tax on rooms and tourism services. This is a dedicated, earmarked tax levied specifically so that tourism activities will provide the mechanism for their own administration and growth. Tax revenues are put into a separate fund within the federal government's budget and disbursed against requisitions or invoices from authorized personnel within the department.

At early stages of development, however, the tax on rooms and tourism services does not meet all the operating needs of the department. The difference between the collected taxes and the full operating budget is made up by contributions from the private sector. These are handled through a quota contribution plan administered by the commissioners.

Thus, during its startup phase, the tourism agency operates under a combination of government funding through a special-purpose tax and private-sector contributions. Ultimately, this pattern is expected to change. It has been true in every major tourism area which has imposed a so-called "bed" tax that funds generated ultimately exceed current budgets for the tourism agency they support. Uncomfortable friction can be generated when managers of the tourism agency attempt to expand their budgets on a crash basis to use up available funds.

Precautions should be taken by any governmental agency which imposes tourism taxes. On the one hand, the tax should not become punitive. If taxation is too heavy, tourists will be offended. There can be sufficient irritation actually to depress the tourism market. On the other hand, it is sound policy to take precautions which assure that monies collected from tourists are used to develop services and facilities which perpetuate tourism.

As indicated, it is typical that tourism revenues spurt forward and develop surpluses which are beyond the current-year budgets of a tourism agency. When this happens, there has been a temptation to scoop up all the additional funds available and appropriate them into the general fund of the governmental entity, using them to salve the economic sore point which shows the most irritation at the moment. This should not be permitted to happen. Tax rates should be set realistically. Taxes collected should be allocated to the purpose for which they are collected. For an industry as volatile as tourism, tax legislation should also have a provision which permits carryforward of surplus funds from one period to the next.

While it is undesirable to syphon tourism-earmarked funds into other areas, it is even worse to attempt to support a tourism function from general funds. Other governmental agencies, and taxpayers at large, may be reluctant to commit taxes raised from their earnings or properties for services to persons from other countries or areas. Any governmental agency which attempts to support tourism from general domestic tax revenues may be courting trouble.

Another tourism funding principle worth noting is that the private sector, where it exists, should contribute something to the development of its own interests. Conversely, if private industry supported tourism development entirely through its own contributions, this could encourage an attitude on the part of legislators and other government officials which regards the developing industry as a windfall. Legislators are human. They will not respect and support a segment of the economy which does not require some support or sacrifice on their part. Thus, the best method for financing a tourism agency has proven, where feasible, to lie in coordination between governmental contributions in the form of proceeds from a special-purpose tax and private contributions.

ECONOMIC CLIMATE CONTROL

Tourism, by nature, is international. Consequently, the industry is extremely sensitive to fluctuations in the international economy. Thus, host countries may find themselves suffering declines in volume due to circumstances entirely beyond their control.

Further, particularly in a developing area, the host government should recognize that it will be expected to provide a stable, attractive investment environment for its own and foreign capitalists. For most governments in developing areas, this translates to a prerequisite that special efforts be made to support the stability of the nation's currency. Particularly critical is the exchange rate of the host nation's currency with the currency representing its primary source of investment capital.

The exchange rates of currency also affect the potential prosperity of the tourism program itself. Consider the falloff in travel by U.S. citizens following devaluation of the dollar in the early seventies. By comparison, countries which peg their own currency to the value of the dollar have continued to enjoy high rates of tourism.

Another important factor affecting the economic climate of the tourism industry is taxation. Many emerging nations have assumed mistakenly that it was essential to enact major tax concessions to attract a tourism industry. Many who have done this have triggered adverse domestic reactions which, in turn, have led to enactment of highly unfavorable taxes.

Unreasonable tax concessions are certainly not necessary, but carefully conceived incentives, including tax concessions, are. Stability is equally important as concessions. Investors feel that they must be able to predict the impact of taxation upon their incomes for some time into the future. Thus, the most favorable action which legislators can take might be long-range tax codes including guarantees against retroactive enforcement of new taxes, investment tax credits, and loss carryovers. In today's sophisticated investment climate, foreign investors will value stability as highly as short-term concessions.

Another element affecting the economic climate will be the investment code in the host area. Here again, stability should be the keynote. To attract investment, many host areas have found it necessary or desirable to enact economic incentives.

ECONOMIC INCENTIVES

Economic incentives are a proven method for attracting foreign capital for tourism development. In addition, a climate of economic stability is essential for the incentives to be meaningful. Many investors have become wary of economic incentives which they fear may be revoked at times of political instability or may, for other reasons, be temporary.

As with any other management measure associated with tourism success, it takes careful planning to make effective use of investment incentives. Are incentives needed? Will capital materialize anyway? Will the local business community resent heavy investment by foreigners? Are there ways of assuring that foreign investment will be of a long-range nature? Or, conversely, are there ways of assuring that foreign investors will be on the scene only temporarily?

Answers to all of these questions, and many others, lie in establishing objectives and plans at the outset and then developing economic programs which fulfill them. Where it is determined that foreign capital is essential, many different types of incentives have been offered. One of the most common, of course, is taxation. Developing areas frequently offer either forgiveness or reduction in taxation for a predetermined period. Taxation, however, is only one of several types of economic incentives offered.

Broadly, such incentives frequently include:

- **Fiscal incentives.** These take in special or reduced taxes on investments or income. Also encompassed, however, are relaxation or suspension of import duties and/or suspension or reduction of real-estate taxes. On occasion, governments have established special exchange rates to encourage foreign investment.

- **Loans.** Many governments, some with support of international financing agencies, have underwritten matching loans to correspond with investment of foreign capital.

- **Loan Guarantees.** Where foreign investors have borrowed to help build a tourism industry, host-area governments have frequently cosigned or guaranteed the loans.

- **Subsidies.** Some governments have made outright cash contributions to match capital invested by foreigners in their tourism industry.

A recent international survey by the Organization for Economic Cooperation and Development (OECD) covered 25 member countries. Of these, 18 have offered loans to foreign investors, 12 have used loan guarantees, 13 have provided subsidies, and 12 have had programs for other fiscal incentives.

Economic incentives can be used selectively as well as generally. General economic incentives would apply to investment in tourism development anywhere in a given country or area. Selective incentives would apply to specific types of investment or geographic regions. When used selectively, economic incentives provide an excellent means for stimulating and directing foreign investment in tourism. To illustrate, a number of U.S. cities are using selective incentives to encourage the development of convention and hotel facilities in urban-renewal areas. These selective incentives have included sale of land to developers at below normal market value, reduction or postponement of real property taxes, no-cost provision of ancillary services (parking structures, utilities, etc.), special manpower training programs, and so on.

ECONOMIC INCENTIVE POLICIES

The foregoing types of economic incentives are, in effect, tools for attracting capital. A management challenge in tourism development lies in using these tools to apply just enough leverage to bring in the capital and other financial resources needed for meeting the developmental objectives of the master plan. The amount or degree of incentives utilized will, in general, depend upon the status of tourism in the host area. Also affecting the offering of incentives is the extent of development which has already taken place. In general, the more highly developed the area is at the outset of its tourism program, the lower its capital requirements will be and the lower will be the risk to investors.

Consider: within a relatively developed nation or area, most of the infrastructure which will require high amounts of high-risk capital will probably be in place. A road system is likely to exist. Power, water, sewage, and other necessary utilities will probably exist also. Even if infrastructure facilities have to be expanded substantially, this will still involve less of a risk and smaller amounts of capital than starting from scratch.

As it becomes necessary to attract foreign capital which regards tourism development in the host area as a high-risk investment, the need for incentives increases. Depending upon the nature of the tourism industry being developed and the condition of the area at the time, economic incentives can serve any or all of three major purposes:

1. Governmental incentives can serve to make investments in the area attractive in terms of potential return, both in short-range and long-range earnings.

2. Economic incentives can serve to insure investors against unusually high risks. The logic here is straightforward: if no tourism industry currently exists, the ability of the area to attract people and support the industry is open to some degree of question. Assurances and incentives would be designed to help attract capital to investments which would otherwise be considered questionable.

3. Incentives can help attract investment to projects which are clearly uneconomical. Suppose, for example, tourism is being developed from scratch in an area. There are no roads or other utilities. This newness, in itself, generally means that tourism will start on a small scale and build up gradually. Clearly, something must be done to compensate lenders or investors for the capital needed to generate growing tourism activity.

An excellent example of the use of incentives, including government participation, to offset uneconomic investments is seen in the program launched by the government of New Zealand. The objective was to disperse tourism into rural areas, outside of the major cities. Recognizing that these rural sites would accommodate relatively small facilities only, the government determined that a major, front-end investment was necessary to create the roads and other infrastructure elements needed to support tourism. The government actually built the essential utility networks and then even developed and operated the hotel facilities.

To demonstrate how economic incentives can make investment in tourism more attractive, consider a simplified example involving the cost and return on capital for a single hotel room. At this writing, a reasonable investment per' room for an international-class hotel is in the neighborhood of $40,000. These costs might be accumulated as follows:

Land	$ 4,000.
Equipment and furnishings	6,000.
Building	30,000.
Total	$40,000.

The impact of economic incentives on such an investment is illustrated in Figure 9-2. Table A at the top of Figure 9-2 lists the assumptions about available incentives. Table B shows impact of these incentives upon return on gross assets (ROG) for a $40,000 segment of an investment in a hotel.

In implementing a master plan for tourism development, then, early attention and priorities should be accorded to studying investment needs and developing investment codes which deal with the realities of capital requirements for the area.

THE INVESTMENT CODE

The investment code is a body of law. It requires careful drafting and strong legislative support if it is to inspire the confidence necessary to attract capital. Because it is a body of law, an investment code is often full of legislative compromise. The wording can be vague. The provisions can be complex. Investment objectives can actually be more difficult to reach if bureaucratic red tape is written into the investment code. In short, the investment code is not only a necessary body of law, but it is a body of law which must be simply drafted and usable.

Therefore, the investment code should be as complete and explicit as possible. It should tell investors what applications must be made, to whom. Limitations in terms of size of investment, timing, documentation, and content should be stated clearly. For example, applications for investment incentives under investment codes frequently require submission of such documenta-

TABLE A	Without Incentives	With Incentives
Depreciation		
Equipment and Furnishings	10%	10%
Buildings	1¼%	8⅓%
Taxes on Income	33%	33%
Subsidy on Prime Costs (Excluding land)	—	15%
Reserve for Replacement Fund— Per Room	$300	$300

The effect of applying the foregoing incentives, assuming gross operating profit of $6,000 per room, will be observed in the following calculations:

TABLE B	Per Room	
	Without Incentives	With Incentives
Gross Operating Profit	$ 6,000	$ 6,000
Depreciation		
Equipment	$ 600	$ 600
Buildings	375	2,500
Total Depreciation	$ 975	$ 3,100
Profit before Income Taxes	5,025	2,900
Provision for Income Taxes	1,654	957
Net Income	$ 3,366	$ 1,943
Add Depreciation	975	3,100
Deduct Reserve for Replacements	(300)	(300)
Cash Flow	$ 4,041	$ 4,743
Gross Assets	$40,000	$40,000
Deduct Direct Subsidy	—	5,400
Net Assets	$40,000	$34,600
Return on Net Assets	10.1%	13.7%

It should be noted that in the foregoing example, the return is improved by 3.6 percentage points, or better than 35 percent even without gearing (leveraging) considerations. Appropriate methods of financing may have a material impact on return on equity and serve as another — and very meaningful — form of incentive.

Figure 9-2. Impact of incentives upon hotel investment.

tion as feasibility studies, cash flow projections, architectural plans, cost estimates, and construction schedules. If the government will be, in effect, entering into a partnership with the applicant, financial statements of investors may be required.

The investment code should also delineate any constraints clearly. These could involve geography or time. Geography constraints would deal with areas in which investments must be made to qualify for incentives or special treatment. Timing constraints would generally be keyed to schedules within the tourism master plan. For example, if a plan covers a five-year period, incentives may diminish toward the end of the period in anticipation of completion of part of the plan.

It is a sound practice for each item of investment legislation of this type to have a definite termination date. In this way, all parties know where they stand. If the host-area legislature wishes to continue an incentive program, it is clearly understood that a further, definitive commitment is essential. Similarly, investors know, usually through specific provisions guaranteeing their investments against retroactive taxation, that they will be able to operate under stated conditions for a given period of time.

Direct and Indirect Use of Incentives

In addition to establishing the types of parameters described above, an investment code should also spell out all taxes, duties, and conditions applicable to tourism ventures. In general, the government can approach the matter of investment incentives directly or indirectly. This applies for all four types of economic incentives described earlier — loans, loan guarantees, subsidies, or fiscal measures (including taxes).

Direct loan incentives would involve commitment of funds under the control of the local government or quasi-governmental agency. These could include resources of local banks or financial institutions. It could also be possible for the local government to secure developmental loans from an international financial agency and, in turn, lend money on some sort of sharing formula to investors in its tourism industry.

Indirect assistance to lenders would center around such measures as guaranteeing or cosigning loans by governmental or other agencies. In addition, to attract the funds, it is possible for the host area to arrange for or provide insurance which, in effect, guarantees the safety of foreign investments. Frequently, local governments charge lenders and, through repayment schedules, borrowers for this insurance coverage. Where this is done, it is possible to devise financing programs which become largely self-funding. For example, the State of Maine charged interest on loans as a fee for guaranteeing investments. Such fees are kept low enough, usually a fraction of 1 percent, so that they are commercially attractive. Revenue from the fees, in turn, is rotated into a budgetary account which replenishes capital invested in tourism development by the state. Thus, through the insurance mechanism, tourism development becomes largely a self-funding program. (This remains a creative example of financial incentives even though the State of Maine, at this writing, recently abolished its Department of Tourism.)

Where loans or loan guarantees are concerned, the investment code should be as explicit as possible, covering such topics as interest rates, repayment or amortization incentives, repayment schedules, percentages of equities required by foreign investors or local citizens, limitations on size of investment, and so on.

The same should apply for direct subsidies by the local government. Subsidies, too, can be direct or indirect. An example cited, where land is made available within urban renewal areas at less than market value, is an indirect subsidy. Direct subsidies are also possible. The example of the parking structure built at city expense adjacent to a downtown hotel illustrates a direct subsidy.

Tax and other fiscal incentives require the greatest sophistication in delineation and structuring. Broadly, taxes involve the income of investors, the real estate utilized, and the value of improvements upon property. In today's international financial marketplace, it is essential that an investment code incorporate some sort of "tax package" which covers the full impact upon the earning power of an investment. Governments themselves have become both industrious and creative in defining new ways of taxing income and revenue. In different parts of the world, taxes cover income, real estate, personal property, sales, use of facilities, luxury, business licensing, and import duties.

Years ago, it was possible to attract industry or tourism through income-tax incentives alone. Ultimately, investors realized that delays or forgiveness in income taxes took place chiefly during the developmental periods when they were experiencing operating losses.

Today, if an area wants to attract investment through tax incentives, it is necessary to consider the total impact of taxation from the standpoint of the investing business. It may be necessary, for example, to make available special import exemptions during the construction period and to adapt income-tax incentives to periods when income is acutally anticipated. As another device, many areas are finding it desirable to specify that hotels and other tourist facilities in which foreigners own a share be built on leased land. In this way, taxation is for the use of the land rather than for full ownership, minimizing tax rates.

In today's marketplace, investors realize that the local government must support and expand its own functions as a tourism industry develops. Investors are looking for realistic tax structures. They are aware that concessions can become so great that they become untenable for the local government and bring on punitive measures.

Many models for investment codes exist. Sources of help are also plentiful. The same applies to sources for investment assistance. In many cases, the same international agency, such as the World Bank, the Agency for International Development, or the Organization for Economic Cooperation and Development, can provide information and assistance associated with both lending and drafting of suitable investment codes.

In other instances, the authors have recommended fiscal incentives which have been tailored to the particular situations of areas and countries as an integral part of conceptual planning. Such "made-to-order" codes are most effective, matching what needs to be done with what can be done in a given set of circumstances.

SYNOPSIS

If a tourism program is to succeed, responsibility for success must be assumed by some entity. This organization should have a charter and resources appropriate for its mission. Because tourism cuts across so many facets of governmental jurisdiction, many areas and countries have established special departments or agencies to manage and coordinate tourism programs. Such agencies generally assume functional responsibility for tourism-related activities and serve as coordinators with governmental entities with jurisdiction in other areas. Depending on the political situation in the country or area, the tourism entity may be a governmental department, a quasi-governmental agency

chartered and supported by the government but operating outside its organizational structure, or a private-sector organization
with government recognition and support. Considerable amounts
of power and money are brought to bear in implementing a
tourism program. Whatever organizational approach is used,
therefore, it is important to incorporate safeguards into the rules
under which the tourism entity exercises its authority and responsibilities. These principles are illustrated through a description of
a hypothetic, quasi-governmental agency established to implement a tourism master plan and assume responsibility for
tourism operations in a developing nation. The head of this
agency is at the same level as the minister of finance for the
country. This serves to establish a liaison for applying the
minister-level coordination and support needed to implement
tourism programs. The agency has separate departments for
planning, development, marketing, education and training, and
legal and administration services. One of the responsibilities of
this agency is to counsel the government on programs for
economic incentives which will enhance the ability of the country to attract investment capital. A wide variety of incentive
techniques, ranging from tax exemptions to loans or loan
guarantees, are discussed.

REVIEW QUESTIONS

1. Discuss the reasons for dual functions of a typical tourism
agency, identifying the "line" responsibilities in tourism areas
and the coordinating role assumed in relations with other government departments or agencies.

2. Identify and discuss two economic incentives which can be
used to attract foreign capital to a tourism development
program.

3. Describe the need for and value of political stability in encouraging investment in tourism development.

4. Describe the need for long-range assurance that legislation
covering investments of foreign capital will not be changed suddenly and unexpectedly.

5. This chapter describes the organization and operation of a
quasi-governmental agency with tourism responsibility. Given
the same circumstances as those set forth, describe and explain
the differences which could exist if a decision had been made to
establish a private-sector agency to handle this function.

10

ECONOMIC PLANNING

STARTING POINT: A REALISTIC PERSPECTIVE

There is frequently a strong tendency to assume that economic planning for tourism requires, invariably, a scheme for maximizing revenues. This may, in fact, be the case. But, it may also be true that a particular area, for all of the reasons dealt with in the discussion on master planning, may be best served by modulating the size and economic impact of tourism development. Factors can range all the way from availability of capital, to world trade position, to concerns over social and cultural heritage. The economy itself may serve to modulate fiscal planning. For example, it may be decided that the inflationary impact of tourism, if allowed to get out of hand, could upset the cost of living and the very ability to survive for some segments of the economy and population.

It may be more true in the economic area than in any other that failure to plan and control can, in itself, represent a *de facto*

126

decision to let development run its own course. In effect, this leaves the fate of an entire sector of the economy in the hands of promoters or private-sector developers with little stake and probably little interest in the impact of tourism.

In considering the economics of tourism, certainly far from the least of its attractions as a growth industry is that it represents "instant money." Business is chiefly on a cash basis. Revenues are realized immediately by local businesses. These revenues can be related directly to jobs and salaries for local residents.

Conversely, inventory problems and planning lead times are far less severe with tourism as an industry than, for example, with a manufacturing enterprise. A manufacturer must frequently order raw materials well in advance and keep these for anticipated demands. After products have been made, it can be literally months before revenues are realized. In a tourism facility, inventories are usually small. Turnover tends to be relatively quick. For example, food tends to be ordered on a day-to-day or week-by-week basis. In most tourist facilities this is the major inventory expense. Thus, there is a close, healthy relationship between cash flow and operating expenses.

For a developing area, tourism can also have a major impact on balance of payments. For the most part, people who have the means to become tourists bring "hard" currency into an area. This can be significant. The availability of this foreign exchange can contribute directly to an area's development by providing the means to secure manufactured and consumer items from abroad.

UNAVOIDABLE RESPONSIBILITY

Because of all of these factors, economic planning — except in extreme, isolated instances where ownership of vast areas is in private hands — is an unavoidable government responsibility. Failure to recognize this responsibility can, as discussed earlier, leave the country or area economically adrift.

Given that economic planning is logically a government responsibility, the next vital characteristic is that this activity must be both broad in scope and extensive in content. Partial planning or incomplete planning for tourism-related elements of the economy can create a false sense of security. This, in its ultimate impact, can be worse than no planning at all.

127

For example, in allocating the funding for construction of a large stadium or convention meeting facility, government officials are committing their area to the potential impact of large crowds. Typically, convention business brings with it a certain, unavoidable level of commercialization and noise. In addition, the investment needed for a major facility of this type serves automatically to involve the area in seeking continuing, high volumes of this type of business. In turn, support for conventions demands, today, high-rise hotels and facilities for large dining and social functions. Also prerequisite are capabilities for handling large crowds at airports or other terminals and corresponding capabilities in roads and ground transportation. Thus, it is impossible simply to say it would be a good idea to have a stadium or convention hall as a means for building a tourism industry. If this were done, the act would represent a decision by default to proceed with all of the other implied commitments.

The point is that economic decisions have a way of snowballing. Having decided to make an investment, it then becomes necessary to protect it. If the accompanying or continuing implications are not thought of in advance, they can represent expensive or disastrous surprises.

TOURISM'S IMPACT—A SPECIAL DIMENSION

These considerations are particularly important in economic planning for tourism because of the previously cited multiplier effect implicit in income from this industry. Specifically, tourism-derived income, because of its service nature, recycles through the economy with a multiplier effect. This multiplier factor is variable and, as part of economic planning, should be determined for the individual area or country.

In general, the more self-sufficient an area is, the greater the multiplier effect will be. Conversely, the more dependent an area is upon imports of goods and services, the more of its tourism revenues it will have to export.

Thus, it would be possible for an area to experience a multiplier effect of one or possibly fractionally less. This would occur, for example, when an area was forced to send tourists across the border to a neighboring state or country for given types of entertainment or services. Suppose, for example, an area had insufficient ground-transportation facilities and had to engage buses from a neighboring city or state for tours or special transportation requirements. The payments of rent for the equipment and the salaries of operators are exported out of the area. The term, "leakage," is used to describe this type of loss.

Conversely, the more services that can be performed by area residents, the larger the recycling impact of tourism revenues will be. Tourism income recycles, for example, through purchases in gift shops. If the items sold in gift shops are made in the area, the money recycles a second time to pay the artisans. If the items are made from native materials, there is still another recycling. The same applies to all services consumed by tourists. Salaries to waiters in a dining room represent a recycling of tourist income from the hotel to the personnel involved. Then, if the food is locally grown, there is an additional recycling into the agriculture of the area.

It should be part of the economic planning process to identify this multiplier factor and to regard tourism as an opportunity to build other services or industries within the area itself. Clearly, this scope of planning must be a governmental function.

There are many schools of thought and many approaches used in projecting revenues which a tourism industry will produce. This is frequently done by building questionnaires into documents which tourists complete — such as exit visas. Typically, there is a form which asks the tourist a few basic questions: the number of persons in the party, length of stay, modes of travel for arrival and departure, points of entry and departure, and estimates of the amount of money spent.

It can also be effective to take available information generated in the normal course of conducting tourism business and extend or project these to estimate revenue volumes. For example, bank clearings for foreign exchange, travelers' checks, and sales tickets against foreign credit cards can be excellent indices of tourism activity. It may not be possible to project total expenditures from these data. However, since the data are available continuously, they do have obvious comparison value. It can be meaningful to note, for example, that foreign exchange is down by 10 percent today as compared with yesterday, or that it has spurted by 30 percent as the peak tourism season approaches.

Another valuable yardstick can be data filed by hotels paying occupancy taxes. Such information makes it possible to determine how many people are using rooms in hotels or other facilities which cater to tourists. Given the regular and reliable availability of these data, it becomes possible to derive a multiplier of room rents as an estimate of tourism revenue. In general, it is desirable to find some way to relate each day spent by a tourist or family in the area to some projected amount of revenue. This is done simply by coming up with a gross figure and then dividing it by the number of tourists who visited the area. The visitor-level figures, of course, are derived from airlines and other carriers as well as from immigration reports.

Given a determination that to build upon an existing nucleus of tourism business, a good starting point is to identify the current visitor mix and place a value on the revenues they are generating. By extending the analysis of revenues per tourist, it becomes possible to project, as close as these things can be projected, the revenues an area can anticipate if marketing goals are met.

THE ECONOMIC PLANNING PROCESS

This discussion assumes that an area undertaking tourism development has the necessary economic planning mechanisms and procedures in place or has arranged to implement them. Given the existence of an economic planning function, it is important for managers and decision makers associated with tourism to understand and to be able to relate the special requirements and characteristics of tourism planning to the overall economy.

Typically, economic planning for tourism will be carried out in three phases:

1. Projections of investments and costs

2. Estimates of revenues

3. Cost/benefit analyses.

Projections of Investments and Costs

This phase of economic planning consists largely of assigning realistic budget allocations to the adopted elements of the master plan. Economic planners must obtain advice from engineers, architects, operations managers, accountants, and others. The figures which result should show a schedule of expenditures for implementing the facilities and capabilities specified in the master plan.

An important note: this phase of economic planning should cover both public and private-sector requirements. It is important to recognize, when doing economic planning, that one cannot function without the other. It is useless, for example, to expand an airport without corresponding expansion of other guest facilities. The master plan identifies necessary accomplishments and contributions of each sector.

The result of this phase of economic planning is to create the capital budgets necessary to implement the master plan. An important part of this process lies in locating sources of needed capital and verifying availabilities. It can be one thing to determine how much it will cost to build all of the facilities needed to implement a master plan and quite another to verify that the money will be available as and when needed. Thus, this phase of economic planning involves extensive conferences and, ideally, commitments between governmental departments, private-sector companies engaged in or supporting tourism functions, bankers, the economic arms of the government itself, and others. The end product of all of these activities should be a program for funding the master plan.

Estimates of Revenues

The estimating of revenues to be generated by the tourism industry should actually take place concurrently with development of the capital plan. The two planning phases are closely interdependent. Almost without exception, capital commitments will require reliable projections of income.

Bear in mind that the steps leading up to the preparation of the conceptual plan included projections of revenues based upon assumptions of expenditures for facilities and services. During the economic portions of master planning, the process moves forward to identify the exact sources of capital for tourism development. It is also necessary, in attracting and justifying the investment of capital, to identify which entities will realize how much revenue. This must be done for every component of facilities or services included in the master plan.

Thus, for example, it is not enough simply to say that an airport will require a gross amount of capital investment. Rather the airport facility itself must be broken down into components. One of the components might be a restaurant and bar. During economic planning, it is necessary to identify the costs to an operator for leasing and equipping this facility. Having done that, it then becomes necessary to project, with some reliability, the revenues which could be anticipated by the operator of the facility. These projections must be carried to a level of detail which makes them believable if reputable organizations are to be encouraged to bid for contracts.

For private-sector investors, this detailing is necessary as a basis for justifying capital investments. The same, generally, is true for the government. Government officials must know how much revenue private-sector business will generate so that tax income can be forecast realistically. In total, the process of estimating tourism revenues produces what can be considered a highly detailed operating budget. As this analogy implies, estimates of revenues include both gross and net amounts, with operating expenses being forecast and taken into consideration. The final result of this phase of the economic planning process is what amounts to a *pro forma* set of projected income statements.

Cost-Benefit Analyses

This phase of the economic planning process uses outputs from the first two phases. The idea is to look at the investments required and determine whether projected income justifies them. This is a straightforward decision-evaulation process. Activities of this phase must be carried out in sufficient detail to cover each significant element of the master plan. Further, these projections must be organized and presented in formats and with content which are meaningful to the large number of individual investors and participants who will become associated with the program. For example, projections of income and capital requirements for hotels should be stated in terms which are compatible with standard charts of accounts used in the industry. The same should be true for restaurants, airlines, and other participating segments. Governmental projections must be compatible with existing budget structures.

When complete, the economic plan should serve as the basis for serious, extensive review which leads to investment decisions and commitments. Throughout this consideration, the interdependent nature of tourism development should be a guiding and controlling factor in all of the work done and agreements reached. Economic planning for tourism involves many contingencies. Very few parts of a tourism industry can function independently. Thus, the models and projections which emerge from this process will be highly complex. They will also be voluminous because it is necessary to show each part independently while relating all of the parts together in an overall plan and projection.

Developmental and operating considerations associated with some of the more important of the diverse parts of the tourism industry are covered in the series of chapters which follows.

SYNOPSIS

Economic planning is an important facet of tourism master planning. In establishing an economic plan, it is valuable, at the outset, to establish a perspective to determine what, realistically, can be achieved. For example, there is a tendency to assume that a goal of tourism development is to maximize income. This is not necessarily the case. Physical, cultural, or resources constraints may call for less-than-maximum growth. Failure to study the economic situation and establish controls represents an effective default, placing the tourism portion of the economy in the hands of promoters and private-sector developers. To avoid such loss of control, it is essential that public-sector officials recognize their exposures and responsibilities and protect their area through careful economic planning. Effective exercise of these responsibilities calls for establishing an orderly economic planning process. The process recommended is carried out in three stages: 1) Projections of investments and costs, 2) Estimates of revenues, and 3) Cost/benefit analyses.

REVIEW QUESTIONS

1. Describe the potential consequences of failure to establish an economic plan in an area undertaking a program of tourism development.

2. For your area or one with which you are familiar, describe strengths and economic-planning weaknesses which you have

observed or read about. Discuss steps which could have been taken to build further upon strengths or to avoid or correct problems resulting from planning or decision weaknesses.

3. Describe the requirements and uses for a projection of investment requirements and costs for a tourism-development program.

4. Describe the processes used to estimate revenues from tourism. Discuss the relationships between revenue projections and cost estimates.

5. Describe the preparation and use of cost/benefit analyses as a prerequisite for economic planning for a tourism program.

11

LAND ACQUISITION AND SITE DEVELOPMENT

THE MOST CRITICAL RESOURCE

Land is the most critical single resource to be managed in a program of tourism development.

There are other prerequisites, of course. There is climate. There are oceans, rivers, or natural lakes. But these other natural elements are not subject to management to the same degree as land. Such natural resources enhance the attractiveness, usability, and even the value of land. But capitalizing on these assets still requires skillful acquisition and management of land.

Even manpower can be developed or imported. Once committed, manpower can be retrained or rechanneled. But land, for the most part, cannot be manufactured. Misused land can cause irreversible damage.

Because the stakes are so high, land utilization tends to provide the most creative challenge and the greatest exposure to error and loss associated with the development of a tourism industry. Thus, in planning for and developing a tourism program, land planning and utilization can be the most important single responsibility. Its management calls for application of a cross section of skills and disciplines, some highly technical and little understood. Conceptually, however, land, its development, and utilization are easy to understand and are very much worth the investment of management time needed to study and arrive at decisions concerning disposition and development.

IDENTIFYING DESIRABLE LAND

Management-evaluation criteria covering desirability and suitability of land for tourism development include:

- Location
- View
- Environmental suitability
- Terrain
- Availability
- Usable area.

Location

If tourists or construction and support personnel cannot get to a given site with some predefined level of convenience and assurance, its usability in a tourism program is doubtful. This does not mean that every facility or attraction must be astride a superhighway or adjacent to an airport. It does mean that it is necessary to think carefully about how land will be used and by whom and to assure convenience of each location.

The greater the amount of use anticipated, the more accessible a site should be in terms of both convenience and proximity to housing and major transportation facilities. Thus, if plans call for a large theme park, it is essential that transportation and accommodations facilities be close at hand. By contrast, many resorts catering to an exclusive clientele have been successful in locations with restricted accessibility. To illustrate, there are resorts specifically for persons arriving by private aircraft, boat, or even four-wheel drive vehicles.

When an attraction with strong appeal exists at a site whose location is not subject to management control, accessibility may have to be improved. Consider, for example, the many visitors attracted to archeological ruins. Location of such sites is neither controllable nor manageable. To capitalize on their appeal, then, it becomes necessary to manage the factor of accessibility. Mexico has done this, for example, through increases in airline service to Merida, near the archeological sites on the Yucatan Peninsula, and through construction of a first-class road from Mexico City to the ruins of Teotehuacan.

Proximity between accommodations facilities and major attractions can be a critical consideration in evaluating location. Beaches must be adjacent or comfortably close to hotels depending on them as visitor attractions. Golf courses should be adjacent to the resorts with which they are associated. Restaurants and shops should be conveniently accessible from accommodations facilities.

In evaluating location, a convenient approach is to think through or simulate the experience of the visitor unfamiliar with the destination. Any access pattern which is inconvenient to a tourist should, unless there are understandably extenuating circumstances, lead to challenging or disqualification of a location.

View

An attractive view can provide anything from enhancement to the basic stock-in-trade for an accommodation facility or attraction. Most tourists are attracted to destinations at least partly for an experience involving natural beauty and serenity. There are, of course, other attractions. For each destination, the importance of view should be evaluated and related to location of facilities.

For example, one of the authors was asked to consult recently on development of a major resort utilizing a mountain lake of great beauty. Local officials had begun implementation of a plan which called for construction of a network of hotels, roads, and other facilities all around the perimeter of the lake. The consulting study determined the existing, unspoiled view provided one of the chief potentials of this prospective resort. Accordingly, the plan was modified: all accommodation facilities were placed on one side of the lake, leaving the view permanently unspoiled.

Environmental Suitability

Tourism facilities must use, but should not abuse, their environments. This is why, increasingly, governmental and tourism agencies in all parts of the world are insisting upon environmental impact studies as prerequisites to development of land resources.

A tourism facility is a heavy user of water. (See Chapter 13.) Prodigious volumes of sewage are generated. Appearances are altered substantially. Impacts of tourism development should be projected and controlled.

At the same time, it should be recognized that the environment itself must provide some key elements for the success of a tourism venture. These may include sunshine, climatic temperatures, surf, snow, hills, beaches, isolation, urban facilities, water, natural drainage, vegetation, and other features. Evaluation of the environment should relate directly to the planned use for each site. Comparing plans for a given facility with the environment into which it will be placed can be a high-yield activity for managers and/or decision makers.

Terrain

The terrain of land relates to environmental suitability of a site. But terrain is sufficiently important economically and for engineering purposes to warrant special consideration. The importance of drainage has already been noted. In addition, terrain affects the cost of excavation and construction. It is possible to have a potentially excellent site which cannot be developed economically because of the costs of excavation, grading, or construction. Seismic and geological factors can also provide either support or disqualification for developmental plans. In general, terrain should support and enhance the designated use of land.

Availability

Before land can be used, it must be acquired. Laws and customs governing ownership and acquisition of land vary widely in different countries. As part of each master-planning effort, consideration should be given to the cost, timing, procedures, politics, and public reactions which may be associated with acquisition of necessary land. Anticipated ease of acquisition can affect site selection.

Usable Area

Tourism development implies growth. Growth, in turn, requires room for expansion. Land allocation for development of tourism facilities should provide sufficient area for each of the service and/or support functions involved. This element of land-use planning, in particular, calls for experience and expertise. Initial studies and recommendations should be provided by experts. Managers and tourism decision makers can then checkpoint these recommendations through comparisons with land-use programs at other, similar destinations.

LAND-USE RELATIONSHIPS

The relationships between land and the uses to which it will be put can be critical in master planning. In general, land allocation must conform to projected visitor experiences. The process builds from the projections of accommodations and activity patterns established during conceptual planning. From there, land is allocated according to the factors described above, plus additional considerations which include:

- Convenience of access between living, recreational, and other activity areas
- Relationships between activities and their essential supporting services
- Relationships between tourism and related commercial areas
- Availability or practicality for providing utilities
- Housing for or accessibility by local workers
- Distances between living areas and prime attractions.

To illustrate these principles, consider land-use patterns established in most modern, popular resorts. These are based on the fact that people want to be able to walk from their living quarters to recreational facilities. So, pedestrian patterns and walking distances tend to govern land-use feasibility in resort planning.

Within this general constraint of distance there is also a factor of logic: recreational facilities which require the same support capabilities should be near each other. Following this rationale, locker rooms and showers are generally found at a hub of facilities which can include a golf course, tennis courts, swimming pool, gym, and health club.

Similarly, eating and shopping facilites are generally near each other. Where these are not adjacent to living areas, they are frequently near parking lots or bus transportation points.

Plans for acquisition of land and allocation of its use should reflect orderly patterns of study and decision making. Where alternate uses of land are considered, determinations can be made on the basis of tradeoffs between visitor experiences and the interests of the people and economy of the host area.

A BIG RESPONSIBILITY

Acquisition and disposition of land invariably invokes the elements of sentiment and emotion. Land, by its nature, is closely enmeshed with the rights and traditions of the people who reside on or near any specific location. Thus, any change can be traumatic. And, in almost any area, tourism will represent major changes.

Thus, one of the key ingredients for any program of land acquisition and development should center upon accomplishing the greatest good for the greatest number of people indigenous to the area. Herein lies a potential source for friction. Tourism facilities tend to be developed, at least in part, by investors and experts of various disciplines. The concentrations and concerns of these groups can be, and frequently are, at odds with those of current and historic users of land.

This is why the government's role in the acquisition and development of land for tourism utilization is critical. Special relationships and programs are frequently necessary to the acquisition of land. These are built upon realization of the fact that many special-interest groups within both government and the private sector will be involved in using land allocated for tourism. To illustrate, without some overview and control, governmental agencies responsible for highways and parks could be at odds about the allocation and utilization of land. The parks people want to maximize recreational use. Highways and traffic specialists want to expedite the movement of people and vehicles. The parks people stress scenic beauty; the highways people live in a world of steel and concrete. Both are necessary. A balance must be established.

To strike the necessary balance between elements of government and between the private sector and governmental agencies, a special agency is frequently formed. This can either be an arm of government or a quasi-governmental organization backed by enabling legislation which makes possible the condemnation, acquisition, and development of land. In a number of programs with which the authors have been associated, these agencies are known as "tourism land boards." In practice, the people who implement the programs of the land board are usually the same as those involved in feasibility and land allocation studies during conceptual and master planning. Thus, land planning, acquisition, and development should, and usually do, form a continuity.

Some of the most successful international tourism destinations have used this approach. As already cited, local land boards have been established in such places as Tahiti, Fiji, and India. In Hawaii, a Land Use Commission establishes broad land-development regulations and controls according to utilization categories — urban, agricultural, conservation, and rural. In urban areas, county governments have further jurisdiction over land utilization through planning and zoning legislation.

The important thing is that the planning-allocation continuity established by such agencies strikes a balance between requirements and aspirations of the local population while still providing attraction and services to tourists. Some type of compromise is generally necessary to achieve this balance. This compromise lies between the interests and advantages of local residents on the one side, and the convenience, comfort, and beauty provided to tourists on the other. The earlier this balance and accord can be struck, the better a tourism program will fare.

DEVELOPING LAND RESOURCES

Everybody has heard horror stories about real-estate development. There was, for example, the case of the high-rise building planned without any elevators. Then there was the post office without a letter drop.

Tourism facilities are probably more susceptible to oversight or blunder in their design than most commercial structures. For example, literally scores of resort hotels have been designed so that the swimming pools are in the shade, frustrating tourists who are spending large sums of money to get sun tans. There have been a number of facilities in which designers have overlooked the need for steam connections to be brought into the kitchens. One facility designed for convention business was constructed with a lobby which had space for only eight or 10 people to stand at the registration desk. In this same facility, a series of meeting rooms was designed partially for banquet use. However, it is impossible to get directly from the kitchen to these banquet rooms.

Obviously, if tourism facilities are to succeed, they must be designed for the convenience of guests and for practical use by the staff. Thus, in creating and evaluating plans, it is necessary, always, to think about and reach decisions on the basis of the projected experiences of the people who will be spending money and those who will be working to provide services to them.

The earlier this planning takes place, the better. For example, it is comparatively inexpensive, before a hotel is built, to install connections which make it possible for guests to turn off their television sets from bedside. However, after the facility is built, such alterations become extremely expensive.

Similarly, in the course of developing a facility, compromise and redesign are frequently necessary. When this is done, the same criteria should be applied as for the initial design. For example, in approving development plans for a convention-oriented hotel, the owners found construction costs were over budget. They were able to complete the facility with funds available by eliminating one large ballroom. When the hotel was finished, it turned out that the deleting of this ballroom from the plans made it unsuitable for large conventions. Thus, the facility was effectively isolated from a major portion of its market. The point: facilities which actually become the tourism industry must be designed with specific purposes in mind throughout their planning and development. These facilities must fit a plan of use which is developed realistically at the outset and followed to completion.

SYNOPSIS

Land is the most critical resource subject to management control within a tourism-development program. One of the key management challenges lies in identifying land which is desirable for tourism use. Factors considered include location, view, environmental suitability, terrain, availability, and usable area. Also considered are conditions bearing upon uses of the land. These include convenience of access between living and activity areas, relationships between activities and supporting services, relationships between tourism and commercial areas, utility services, housing or transportation for local workers and distances between tourism accommodations and prime attractions. To exercise the important responsibilities of land allocation and use, many tourism destination areas establish special land-use agencies responsible for maintaining a balance between service to tourists and protection of the interests of local residents. Officials of these agencies, as well as other involved parties, should exercise special care with controls over tourism development. Because of the nature of tourism itself, development of facilities tends to be more error prone than most commercial projects.

REVIEW QUESTIONS

1. Describe and discuss the importance of location of land as a factor in its selection for use in a tourism program.

2. Explain the rationale for and typical functions of land-use commissions established to acquire and develop land for tourism use.

3. Explain why and how it can be important to cluster recreational areas around the common service facilities they need, such as locating all sports activities around locker rooms and showers. Give another example.

4. Describe how you might go about evaluating the desirability of a parcel of land for tourism development.

5. Using an area with which you are familiar, illustrate and describe the consequences of *either* good or bad land-use planning.

12

TRANSPORTATION

ACCESSIBILITY—A
NECESSITY OF TOURISM LIFE

For tourism to happen, a destination has to be accessible. Arrangements for convenient, comparatively economical travel from origin markets must exist or must be created. The word *must* is worth stressing.

If distances between a destination and its origin markets are more than a few hundred miles, convenient, modern air transportation must be available if a substantial destination is to be developed. The need for air service, in turn, has led major tourism destinations to adopt either or both of these approaches:

1. Arrange for established air carriers to serve a developing destination.

2. Form or expand a national, or flag, airline operated by the government of the country in which the destination is located.

144

In either case — or in situations where an area is served by both flag carriers and others — the objective is the same: to make it possible for travelers to move from home to destination as directly and quickly as possible. Directness and quickness of travel are both important. As tourism spans greater distances, travel time (often to a greater degree than money) generally becomes the controlling factor determining whether tourists from a prime market can spend their vacations at a given destination. People go on vacation to enjoy themselves. They don't have fun while they are sitting on airplanes — or on trains or buses. So, the idea is to bring tourists to the activities which attract them as quickly and directly as possible.

Recognition of these prerequisites for tourism success was one of the driving forces behind the formation of many national airlines. Owning the airline provided routing controls which led to direct service between growing tourism destinations and their prime markets. Another obvious driving force was pride. A sense of national success comes both from ownership of modern airlines and from the ability to control routes and services advantageously.

Demands for direct travel connections can actually play a role in shaping the location of facilities and the allocation of land in a destination. To illustrate, travelers do not enjoy completing a flight of several hours only to find themselves faced with a bus or train ride of several more hours to reach their ultimate destination. So, it is important to think of all of the traveling a tourist will do as part of a single experience. Travel within an area is an extension of the trip from home; and the return trip home is an extension of the travel within the destination area.

MANAGING THE JOURNEY

Thus, the transportation portion of a tourism visit — the journey — is an element which lends itself to separate, direct planning and control. This is done primarily through positioning of gateways used for arrival and departure and routing of ground-transportation networks.

An arrival-departure gateway is the primary element of the staging function, described earlier. Most major gateways are international airports, though railroad stations, bus terminals, or even border-crossing gates could conceivably fit this role. Given

145

tourist distaste for extensive ground travel immediately after a long flight, it has become standard to locate accommodation facilities and some attractions in the vicinity of most gateway airports.

If extensive ground travel becomes part of a stay, additional trips usually begin after a rest period in the gateway area. To the extent possible, ground transportation routings should avoid doubling back through areas already covered. These ground-travel routings should also be designed to bypass areas where the impact of tourism is not wanted. If a decision has been made not to develop tourism in an area, it is best to avoid all exposure.

Where ground-travel opportunities are extensive, two or more gateways can be used in a single journey. To illustrate, it is common for tours of the United States originating in Europe to use Kennedy airport in New York as one gateway and Dulles airport near Washington, D.C., as another. Similarly, tours of California frequently use Los Angeles and San Francisco as gateways.

Since arrival and departure experiences are so critical to enjoyment of a vacation, it follows that the design of facilities and attitudes of personnel at major terminals should be as pleasant as possible. This requirement applies to both government officials and airline personnel.

Separate planning, development, and operating requirements apply to each major mode of tourism transportation — air, private auto, taxi, bus, rail, and ship.

AIR

International tourism is dependent upon efficient, relatively economic airline service. In effect, airlines and destination areas form an inevitable, though sometimes uncomfortable, partnership. Airline fares and airline service represent an important part of the package which a destination area sells to the traveling public.

In addition, the economics of air travel may well become a major concern of the tourism authority at the destination. This is because operation of facilities and services is part of the cost which must be added into the price of an airline ticket. Thus, fees charged to airlines for the use of airports and terminal facilities can have the effect of adding to or diminishing the attraction of the destination. Concessions may be necessary. The need for negotiation is ever-present.

It would be pointless, however, for this book to dwell in detail upon the nature or course of such negotiations, since the airline business itself is so dynamic. Air-fare structures change dramatically from year to year. So do landing fees or terminal costs. Some trends, however, are clear:

- Airlines are continually exploring methods for generating new traffic through the lowering of fares. Excursion and charter fares will undoubtedly continue to proliferate into the foreseeable future.

- Airlines continue to seek incentives or concessions from destinations for the use of terminals, the housing of crews, the purchase of services and materials, or other arrangements.

- Airlines are moving, on a wholesale basis, into the hotel business. This greatly increases the area for cooperation, friction, or demands which destination-area governments and airlines will place upon each other.

Negotiations with airlines should recognize that a carrier must either be subsidized or be fairly well assured of profitable payloads. A commercial air carrier considering service to a developing or emerging tourism area will want a relatively high level of assurance of revenues representing sales of a substantial majority of available seats — or equivalent subsidies. To help achieve a profitable level of sales, airlines generally use a combination of fare structures or travel packages. These can include (but are not necessarily restricted to):

- Full-fare tickets
- Excursion or tour packages
- Group travel plans
- Charter flights.

Full-Fare Tickets

Full-fare tickets are sold largely to business travelers and relatively affluent individuals. These people are unable or unwilling to make the advance commitments usually necessary to qualify for discount fares. On a profitable air route, business travelers paying full fare, ideally, should comprise about 50 percent of the passenger loads carried. Thus, the greater the volume of commerce which exists between a destination area and its primary tourism market, the better the prospects will generally be for establishing a profitable, stable, airline routing. At very least it is necessary to estimate the anticipated volume of full-fare tickets on any route. Typically, these estimates will be based upon existing experience in air travel.

Excursion or Tour Packages

Fare structures covering excursions and tours are designed to appeal to the economy-minded individual traveler or traveling family (as distinct from groups, discussed below). These fare structures generally impose qualifying restrictions or pre-requisites. For example, excursion tickets usually cannot be used on busy weekend days. Another typical prerequisite is that tickets must be purchased seven days before a flight. Cancellations sometimes invoke penalties. Under some structures, dis-counts apply to the spouse and/or children of travelers who are paying full fare.

In general, this class of airline traffic will be highly seasonal, with heaviest volumes conforming to vacation periods in the primary markets. Although volumes in both dollars and seats will usually be lower than for full-fare travelers, this is usually a substantial segment of tourism travel. Some measure of excursion or economy business will usually be necessary if any volume-oriented airline route is to be operated profitably.

Economy or excursion packages are frequently "inclusive." This means that a single tariff or fee includes airline tickets, hotel reservations, all or some meals, rental cars, and possibly admission to some major attractions. To "package" fares in this way, it is obviously necessary to secure agreement and cooperation between airlines, hotels, and other suppliers or vendors of services to tourists. In some instances, the airline, anxious to sell its inventory of available seats, acts as the catalyst, reserving blocks of rooms or cars to go with its tickets. In other instances, governmental or private agencies at destination areas bring suppliers of elements of a "package" together.

Group Travel Plans

A group, under current interpretations of this term within the travel industry, is any number of people, usually 10 or more, sharing travel accommodations so as to qualify for discounts. Groups may be of the "affinity" type, or they may be formed specifically to capitalize on discount opportunities.

Affinity groups, traditionally, have consisted of employees of the same company, members of clubs, associations, or societies. Sometimes these memberships are secured specifically for the purpose of discount travel.

Nonaffinity groups, which may qualify for tariffs which differ from those offered to affinity groups, are formed by carriers or travel agencies. Membership is acquired simply by making reservations for specifically available tours for which block booking has been arranged in advance. The block of space arranged in advance constitutes the membership vehicle.

Group tours are frequently "inclusive." That is, membership in a group of any type implies a precommitment to utilize travel and other accommodations which have been block booked in advance.

Group-travel sales, typically, represent supplementary, or ancillary, income for air carriers. That is, in many instances, a tourism area does not depend upon group travel for its stable, predictable revenues. Rather, group travel is sold as an "extra" to derive additional income from existing facilities.

There are, of course, exceptions. There are individual resorts which cater almost exclusively to the group market.

Charter Flights

Charter flights are, basically, groups which occupy an entire aircraft. The sponsor or contractor, in effect, approaches a carrier with an offer to rent the aircraft for specific flights between pre-identified destinations. A major difference between the charters and groups is that a carrier does not have to be licensed to travel a given route to charter its aircraft to a group for a specific flight. Thus, there are companies which own and operate aircraft without assigned commercial routes. They simply contract to fly groups of persons between desired origin and destination points. Otherwise, charters are highly similar to groups. They can be inclusive or noninclusive. That is, they may cover just travel or may include hotels and other amenities.

PRIVATE AUTOMOBILE

The largest segment of automotive transportation is, obviously, intracontinental. This needs no elaboration. Most auto travel involves a complete journey which begins at home, encompasses one or more destinations, and returns the party to its origin point. For the most part, all transportation takes place with one or more members of the party actually driving the vehicle.

However, there have been innovations through the years which involve automobiles in other modes of tourist travel. For example, the auto-train concept is growing in the United States. Using this service, travelers drive their automobiles onto freight or transport cars linked into the same train on which they have passenger accommodations. This service was initiated with overnight service between Washington, D.C., and Florida. Travelers avoid long, boring drives but still have their own cars available for local vacation use. This concept has spread to several other markets and, at this writing, appears to hold promise for continued growth.

Fly-drive and buy-drive vacation plans have also had varying periods of prosperity and decline in different parts of the world. When European cars enjoyed a greater price advantage than they presently do in the American market, for example, it was relatively popular for manufacturers to package vacations which included factory pickup of automobiles which were used on European vacations, then shipped home. However, this type of sale has declined following devaluation of the dollar which took away some of the advantage of European manufacturers.

Packages including rental of automobiles at destinations have also experienced varying fortunes. Prior to 1973, there had been an extended period of growth for plans which included auto rentals in packages with air fares and some hotel facilities. Following the petroleum crisis of 1973 and the escalation of gasoline prices which ensued, enthusiasm for this type of vacation plan waned, then resurged strongly.

Both the buy-drive and fly-drive approaches to vacation packaging are alternatives which should be kept in mind by planners for tourism industries in areas which lend themselves well to use of private automobiles for vacations.

The basic characteristics and prerequisites for attracting and profiting from automotive travel within any given tourism area present some common denominators which should be considered and evaluated as part of master planning. These include:

- Roads
- Signing
- Visibility
- Parking
- Aesthetics.

Roads

For an area to attract auto tourists, it must have roads which are capable of handling existing and anticipated traffic volumes comfortably and safely. This is not to say that every area must have eight-lane superhighways if it is to attract tourists. The attractiveness of roads for tourists is relative. Consider, for example, the many thousands of tourists who annually drive a partly unpaved road up Pike's Peak in Colorado. The attraction here is scenic. The main management challenge is to avoid overcrowding of highway facilities. The same, in general, is true of the famous 17-mile drive on the Monterey Peninsula in California. This is a winding two-lane road. Yet many thousands of people annually pay for the privilege of driving over this scenic terrain. The toll actually tends to discourage volume, protecting the natural beauty of the area.

Conversely, however, the tourism industry in and around Los Angeles would suffer drastically if the heralded (possibly infamous) freeway system had not been developed.

There are no hard and fast rules. If the automobile figures in tourism-development plans, it is essential that studies be made on volumes and patterns of traffic which are established or can be anticipated. Roads must exist or be planned which can meet these demands.

Worth noting is the fact that it is feasible, sometimes desirable, to invest in and build roads incrementally on a pay-as-you-benefit basis. Two examples illustrate this concept:

- In Fiji, tourism development was limited by the fact that the Queen's Highway, connecting Nadi, the site of the international airport, with Suva, the capital some 200 kilometers away, was a relatively primitive, two-lane dirt road until comparatively recently. The road was paved and widened in three stages under a series of loans from the World Bank, following schedules based on benefits in tourist utilization.

- Substantial increases in tourism activity have resulted from the recent completion of a paved road of more than 1,000 kilometers covering the length of Baja California, in Mexico. Interestingly, Baja built its early reputation on off-road races by four-wheel drive vehicles and motorcycles, adding the road to open the area after it had been publicized substantially by the famous, rugged drivers who ran the annual race. Also interesting is the fact that the segment nearest the U.S. border was paved and widened many years before the rest of the road was undertaken, building up tourism traffic in Ensenada and other northern communities as a prelude to continuation of construction. Along with the road project, the government developed a series of hotels as stopover and destination points for highway travelers.

By contrast, poor or inadequate planning can be disastrous. On one hand, an area can find itself ensnarled in undesirable, unsightly traffic. On the other, if traffic does not materialize to projected levels, roads become lined with deserted, bankrupt business facilities which are equally unsightly and unattractive.

Signing

All over the world, driving tourists have come to rely upon finding signs that they can recognize and understand. In general, roadside signing falls into two broad categories — directional and promotional.

Directional signs are essential. They should be clear, large enough for ready visibility, and placed so as to give drivers enough notice so that they can react. In addition, where foreign travelers are expected, universal picture-type signs should be used. If a substantial portion of tourism volume involves persons who speak a single foreign language, multilingual signing should be provided.

Today, directional signing draws little conflict or contention. Promotional signing, however, can be another matter. All around the world, ecologists and environmentalists are objecting to advertising billboards along scenic highways. They are acting with some reason. Things got so bad in some areas that promotional signs were almost literally obliterating the wonders they were touting.

It is advisable, therefore, to attempt to legislate and operate promotional signing programs so as to strike a valid balance between the need to attract visitors to facilities and the unavoidable degree of ugliness which results. This is largely a matter of taste, making it difficult to be prescriptive in indicating how much promotional signing is needed or how much is enough. From one viewpoint, investors who build major attractions and facilities must promote business. At the same time, if these efforts get out of hand, they can hurt the individual businesses as well as the area as a whole. Further, too much sign-ing along highways can be a safety hazard. Therefore, some way should be found to strike a balance and to maintain it.

Other Highway Factors

It can also be important to recognize that tourists who drive their own cars do so largely to see the countryside. Thus, while it is undesirable to overdo the construction of signs, it is also undesirable to permit natural surroundings to obscure what might otherwise be a breathtaking view. Many roads through beautiful country pass between lines of trees which completely obstruct the view. In other places, motorists risk their lives or the lives of others by attempting to sightsee while driving or by park-ing on inadequate shoulders.

Where a natural view from a highway can enhance the travel experience, provision should be made to do so conveniently. Parking facilities should be established alongside the road at logical points for viewing the scenery. This has been done effec-tively, for example, on Cabot Trail, on Cape Breton Island in Nova Scotia. Another excellent example of capitalizing on natural scenery exists in the three-level highway along the French Riviera. In the United States, almost all highways which cross the Continental Divide provide convenient parking and view points for motorists.

TAXI

In terms of traffic capacity, taxis are, of course, part of the automotive volume. As far as tourists are concerned, however, taxis are something special. Tourists need taxis for the con-venience involved — and also for the security they represent in being able to get about in strange places. Partly because taxis in-volve close personal interaction between passenger and driver, this mode of transportation makes a profound impression on tourists. Taxi service tends to be one of the topics which come up whenever tourists discuss their travels with friends back home. Good taxi service helps the host area; bad taxi service can be harmful.

Master planning for taxi service is relatively straightforward. There should be enough taxis. They should be modern. Drivers should have enough vocabulary in the language of prime tourism markets to understand key words or directions. There should be regulations covering fares; and these should be enforced. In many parts of the world, taxi drivers have gained unsavory reputations. Tourists, therefore, tend to be wary. Anything planners and managers can do to protect and reassure visitors will draw high returns.

Taxi service, when provided at reasonable rates and with high quality, can be a positive force. Many jobs are created for drivers and maintenance personnel. Confidence in taxis also builds confidence for tourists that they can move about. This, in turn, builds traffic to commercial or entertainment attractions.

BUS

Buses bespeak volumes of tourism business. Buses are used because they offer economies of scale and convenience. (It is more efficient to move 40 people in one bus than to tie up a fleet of 10 automobiles.)

In general, an area which is gearing up for a volume-oriented tourism industry must have or be planning for adequate bus-transportation equipment and facilities. Two types of bus-related tourism may have to be considered in master planning:

1. Bus-related activities can initiate and be contained within the tourism area itself. This means the master plan must deal with actual bus equipment, as well as terminal and service facilities.

2. Tours from outside the immediate area may pass through, using facilities and attractions for activities related to visits in nearby or adjoining areas. This type of tourism business involves a need for facilities and capabilities to accommodate the special requirements of large-scale togetherness — people arriving, doing things, checking out, and departing by the busload.

Unlike volume automobile traffic, which has tended to be related recently to travel within the same country or on the same continent, bus requirements apply to international as well as domestic tourism. Buses are expedient methods to handle such necessary functions as ground transfer between airports and hotels, local tours to activity centers or attractions, or intermediate-range tours originating from and returning to an area which serves basically as a tourism destination or staging point. Concerns for bus transportation fall broadly into three categories:

- Facilities
- Logistics
- Equipment.

Facilities

Everybody has heard about, and most tourism managers dread, the experience of busloads of people arriving and attempting to use eating and sanitary facilities which are inadequate. At very least, tourists are exposed to situations which reflect badly upon their total vacation experience. The host area inevitably suffers.

Without going into a lot of technical details, it is essential, today, to forecast the uses of bus transportation and to estimate the volumes of people who will be involved. There must be enough convenient parking for each mass attraction, such as a stadium or theme park, to be visited by buses. There must be service stations, garages, and other facilities to maintain the buses.

Basic as it sounds, the authors have encountered a number of places where inadequate preplanning for bus arrivals has led to inefficiencies and greatly increased out-of-pocket costs for handling this tourism business. For example, many hotels and motels have protected, covered driveways. When these obstruct access to the building by buses, it may be necessary to park the vehicles at a distance, creating extra work in baggage handling and extra confusion in registration, checkout, and departure. In other situations, buses occupy so much parking area that travelers using private automobiles are annoyed and/or inconvenienced. It is important, therefore, to recognize that buses are large. They occupy a lot of room. They need special services. These should be provided for or negative consequences will result.

Logistics

The same, in general, applies to serving and providing for the comparatively large workload surges associated with bus travel. Such functions as registration, admission, checkout, baggage handling, seating, feeding, and others can be severely taxed — sometimes to the point of overburden or failures — if staffing, supply, and service requirements are not anticipated. Planning should recognize that bus arrivals and departures represent special workloads. Provisions should be made to handle them.

Equipment

An area should have enough buses to handle its anticipated traffic. Further, these should be the right kind of buses for the traffic involved.

"Enough" buses implies that a fleet will be large enough to accommodate service requirements, that there will be spare units in case of breakdown, and so on.

It is highly important to have the right kind of equipment for specific tourism service requirements. In general, there are three broad categories of bus equipment. Each is designed to do a specific job. Using equipment for a job for which it is not intended can have highly adverse results. These types of equipment include:

- School-type buses are suitable for short-haul charter work where comfort is not a major factor.

- Transit-type buses are designed for frequent stops, ease of entry or exit, and maximum passenger capacity (including standing room). They usually lack space for parcels or baggage.

- Tourist coaches are designed for longer trips, increased passenger comfort, volume baggage capacity, and some special amenities (frequently including lavatories).

Any or all of these types of equipment may have a valid place in the handling of tourism traffic. At different times, different types of equipment may be used to serve the same groups or people. For example, members of a packaged tour group may require a tourist coach to transport all of the people and their baggage from the airport to a hotel. However, for a one-day outing which occurs as part of a longer stay, a school-type bus may be adequate.

In general, however, tourists come to an area to be comfortable. Bus equipment should be compatible with other types of accommodations. For example, a vehicle to be used for intercity or extensive sightseeing travel should have large luggage compartments which are externally accessible, interior luggage racks, large windows, ventilation or air conditioning, soundproofing, a public address system, adequate lighting, and, in many instances, convenience toilets.

The desirability of first-class bus equipment becomes quite apparent after traveling in a tropical area which has no air-conditioned buses. Such an experience led to a high priority, in a study in India, on the acquisition of air-conditioned buses for the development of tourism facilities in and around new beach resorts.

The caliber of bus equipment should, in general, be comparable with living accommodations. If hotels are economy class, buses can be less lavish. However, if an area is featuring international-class or deluxe-class hotels, buses should be of equal quality.

RAIL

Rail transportation, once a dominant factor in tourist travel, has declined dramatically and continually. Rail travel is still important in some parts of the world, particularly Europe and Japan. In Europe, the railroads, thanks to the Eurailpass, have persisted as a primary method of travel. In Japan, the famous "bullet" trains have become something of a tourist attraction themselves. In Canada, too, rail travel has retained a quality image, though utilization has declined steadily.

A recent study by the authors identified a situation where a rail trip serves as a significant tourist attraction in itself and presents substantial potential for future improvement. This rail line connects Abidjan, the capital of the Ivory Coast, with Ouagadougou, the capital of Upper Volta — a distance of 1,100 kilometers. The railroad provides comfortable seating, sleeping, and eating facilities for a trip which takes some 26 hours, providing a truly unique view of the African countryside and the culture of small towns. Tourists often take the rail line one way and return by air.

The Oslo-Bergen rail route in Norway is another example of a scenic transportation mode.

In the United States, however, rail travel associated with tourism has been allowed to degenerate to an almost-negligible level. There has been some rebuilding in recent years with the advent of Amtrak and auto-train services.

Where quality rail accommodations are available, they can be a major means of promoting regional and interregional tourism, as has been the case in Europe, Japan, and Canada. As a tourism conveyance, a railroad has some important benefits or advantages. Rail travel, for example, can provide attractively priced transportation, can handle large volumes of people for short or medium-range distances with great efficiency, and can provide excellent exposure to scenery and local lifestyle as part of the travel experience. Further, rail depots, with convenient downtown locations, tend to make excellent arrival, departure, and staging areas if they have not been allowed to deteriorate.

Where rail transportation holds some promise, there are a number of special requirements or potential problems to be dealt with:

- Special transportation arrangements may be necessary between the rail depot and major accommodation facilities.

- Where a rail terminal is a port of entry, care must be taken to be sure that there are sufficient baggage handling, customs, banking, and information-dispensing services. In a rail terminal, this can be a problem of a different dimension from an air terminal, since passengers customarily have their baggage with them and may need assistance in moving across platforms.

- Rail depots can provide special problems because of the potential for heavy arrival and departure loads at limited, peak periods. Thus, special bus or taxi dispatching techniques may be necessary.

SHIP

As with trains, ships have become primarily a method for freight transportation. This, too, represents a reversal from the days when ships were the only method available for people to travel across oceans. In those days, shipboard travel became highly stratified, both socially and economically.

More recently, tourism via ship has had a rejuvenation with the advent of relatively short or mid-range cruises. Typically, a cruise ship will have relatively few classes of accommodations. There has been a leveling out in dining and entertainment accommodations for passengers. The range of fares has also narrowed considerably.

Today, market-responsive cruises tend to be relatively short in distance and duration. Thus, the Caribbean, the Mediterranean, the Pacific Coast of Mexico, and the inland passage between Western Canada and Alaska have provided primary routes.

The use of ships also has shown growing potential on an intraregional basis. In some areas, ships provide local transportation through ferry service, as is the case between Seattle and offshore and Canadian islands. In other situations, the experience is more extensive, as with cruises which take overnight or several days down major rivers, such as the Rhine or the Nile. In the United States, an enjoyable trip is experienced by tourists aboard the Delta Queen, a river steamer which plies the Mississippi River between New Orleans and points North.

The basic characteristics of successful cruise or ferry service include:

- Easy-access metropolitan areas as ports of departure
- Comfortable, modern vessels
- Relative proximity to a number of attractions and points of interest, particularly unique areas offering such features as duty-free shopping or casino gaming.

For areas seeking to attract cruises, one of the important things to recognize is that only a segment of the tourism industry will be impacted. There is, for example, very little demand for hotel rooms to be used by passengers of cruise ships. Demand for meals at restaurants is also relatively light, since passengers have frequently prepaid for meals aboard ship. The main potential lies in relatively high volumes of traffic which can be secured for special attractions or activities, as well as for shopping areas.

In general, it is desirable to have some level of activity available close to dockside, since persons who have been at sea for some time usually prefer to walk briefly after disembarking rather than entering immediately into long bus or taxi trips. However, attractions involving relatively short trips from dockside have flourished.

In determining whether ship transportation has any potential for an area, geography and climate are primary concerns and considerations. Generally, a cruise stopover area must be close to a major port of departure. It must also be along a convenient cruise route and have high prospects for favorable climate, as well as the types of attractions described above.

TRAVEL/TRANSFER SERVICES

Transfer and ground travel services associated with arrivals and departures can be the most unpleasant experiences in any travel-oriented vacation. This may be unavoidable. It may, for example, be impossible completely to eliminate lines of immigra-

tion counters and customs facilities or extensive waiting for baggage. In such cases, however, discomfort tends to be multiplied
geometrically. That is, the longer people wait, the more the
unpleasantness of the experience becomes magnified.

The problem is largely one of contrasts. People tend to arrive
in tourism areas in large, well-maintained, attractive aircraft
operated by skilled professionals who function in a competitive
environment. They tend to stay at modern hotels which extend
themselves to accommodate tourists and to make their visits
pleasant. The problem lies in between — in getting from the
transportation to the accommodations. The classic picture of the
tourist arriving in a jet aircraft and then riding to a hotel in a pre-
World War II taxi may be overdone — but not everywhere. For
example, in Tahiti, although taxis are modern, rates double after
11 p.m. This has been perplexing to tourists who find themselves
charged twice as much to return from a late dinner as it cost to
get to the restaurant from their hotel.

The arrival and departure processes, in general, represent
high-yield candidates for management attention. In devoting this
attention, it becomes apparent that problems stem largely from
the nature of the functions themselves. In every other phase of
tourism, there is some aspect of pleasure. People ask: "Did you
have a pleasant flight?" They rarely ask "How was the taxi ride
from the airport?" Every other phase of vacation accommodations represents a major expenditure. Airline tickets are expensive. Hotel and restaurant expenditures tend to be major.
However, limousine or taxi service from the airport to the hotel
tends to be negligible in cost. This may be part of the problem:
costs are not negligible in terms of impact upon the attitudes and
experiences of tourists.

Thus, everything possible should be done to project
workloads and gear up for them. It becomes obvious, for example, that the arrival of a jumbo 747 involves a greater
workload than a 707. Similarly, if planes are arriving every five to
10 minutes through a certain part of the day, this portends
workload problems for baggage handlers, immigration officials,
and customs inspectors.

Then, additional problems can occur after the arriving tourist
clears the airport. Some sensitive attention to the situation can
help. For example, there should be multilingual signs, as appropriate, to indicate bus or limousine routes and destinations,
fares, tipping customs, currency exchange rates, etc. There
should be enough personnel so that individual attention to arriving parties is possible.

Finally, the ground-transportation vehicles themselves deserve some attention. There should be enough vehicles to handle anticipated traffic. These should be modern and maintained in good order. They should be driven by courteous people, with at least some multilingual capability if possible. As appropriate, drivers should point out interesting or important points which the vehicle passes enroute to hotels.

SYNOPSIS

Accessibility is a key requirement for tourism success. Meeting this requirement calls for providing convenient, economic transportation both to and within a destination. The major criteria by which transportation quality is judged are directness and quickness. People want to get to their destinations as soon as possible. They also prefer to avoid stopovers or vehicle changes. Key modes of tourism transportation requiring special planning and operational attention can include air, auto, taxi, bus, rail, and ship.

REVIEW QUESTIONS

1. Identify and discuss at least two reasons — other than profits — which can lie behind formation of a national, or "flag," airline by a country attempting to build tourism volumes.

2. Discuss some consequences which can result if an area has taxi service which tourists feel is inadequate or if a reputation has been developed by taxi drivers in an area for cheating tourists.

3. Explain potential benefits and shortcomings which can result from selection of a tourism area as a stopover for cruise ships.

4. Explain the relative impacts of travel time and money in extending the market potential of a tourism destination.

5. For your area or one with which you are familiar, discuss strengths and weaknesses of bus transportation, including impact on actual or potential revenues.

13

INFRASTRUCTURE

LIFE-SUPPORT SYSTEMS

A successful tourism destination is composed of a series of accommodations and attractions (along with weather) which draw predictable volumes of visitor traffic. To realize the payrolls and revenues which comprise tourism success, it is essential to provide certain necessities of functional subsistence.

Consider: people don't come to a destination to see the airport terminal. If an airport doesn't have a modern passenger terminal, however, the surrounding hotels and attractions may well stand empty. Similarly, streets and highways are needed to get people from the airport to their destination points. There must also be water, power, drainage, sewage capabilities, and other amenities (not the least of which is a system for security).

Collectively, these support services and facilities are known as an infrastructure. By definition, infrastructure comprises the system of services and utilities which are essential to life sup-

162

port. Infrastructure takes in the requirements of local residents as well as tourists. Infrastructure programs, also described widely as public works, are almost invariably a public-sector responsibility.

Possibly one of the classic errors or shortcomings in tourism-development programs lies in insufficient planning or provision for infrastructure components. Somehow, the costs of public-works programs always seem to exceed initial estimates. Failure to look deeply enough at costs and other implications can leave an area without sufficient capacity to support both tourists and its own citizens. In the worst case, tourism attractions and accommodations can stand unused or underutilized if the area does not provide the necessary life-support services.

Conversely, if infrastructure planning and implementation have been well executed, possibly the greatest compliment which can be accorded is that people won't take any notice at all. Infrastructure components, unfortunately, tend to be taken for granted by tourists — and by many governmental or private-sector officials. Strange as it may sound, an objective in infrastructure planning and implementation should be just that — to come up with an overall system which is so good it goes unnoticed. *This is not easy!* Particularly in today's world of environmental emphasis, it takes long planning and much hard work to produce universally acceptable components of a life-support system.

COORDINATED APPROACH

Infrastructure elements cannot be designed and developed in a vacuum. As logical as this may sound, coordination is frequently missing in infrastructure planning. The inherent problem is that different types of people, representing entirely different disciplines from those involved in the other elements of decision making associated with tourism development, play key roles in infrastructure development. Infrastructure planning consists almost entirely of engineering — largely civil engineering — functions. Although engineers are involved elsewhere in tourism-development programs, infrastructure tends to be the primary area where technical considerations control investment policies.

Infrastructure decision criteria, however, tend to be widely divergent. A highway engineer, for example, is typically looking for the best way to move projected amounts of traffic from one place to another. Without guidance, he is apt not to concern himself over minor points like obliterating the view of a beach or ocean. Certainly there is ample proof that, left to their own devices, technicians developing sewage systems are not above using a local river or harbor as a convenient point of disposal. Similarly, it costs more to put power and telephone lines underground than to hang them from poles. In many situations, engineers will not make the decision to bury the lines unless controlling standards are set.

Thus, infrastructure planning and development are team functions rather than specialized assignments which can be delegated and performed in a vacuum. Persons responsible for the ultimate management and success of the tourism endeavor as a whole should examine, in advance, the alternatives for design, routing, construction materials, level of service, and other tradeoffs which invariably go to make up any service-oriented system.

Note the reference to tradeoffs. Some tradeoffs will be necessary in any program. The basic decisions lie in establishing the level of service to be rendered. From there, engineers come up with alternatives. Then the decision makers should re-enter the picture to guide or take part in the selection of the most beneficial alternative. To illustrate, a specification might be that any tourist or visiting businessman should be able to make an overseas telephone call on demand. Later, when the necessary telephone central-office equipment has been designed, it might develop that substantial capital savings can result if the overall system can tolerate waits of up to 10 minutes during peak periods. Management may still opt for immediate service. But the tradeoffs and criteria should be known — and such decisions should not be made by engineers.

This discussion will not attempt to address the technical considerations which must be dealt with in planning and providing infrastructure services. The major areas of infrastructure concern should, however, be understood by anyone who is in or about to enter the field of tourism planning and management. Therefore, the discussion which follows deals with service levels and key decision criteria associated with the most important areas of infrastructure requirements.

WATER

Obviously, potable water is an essential for any economic development involving people. Major tourism development cannot take place without a high-volume water system. Particularly where an area has been relatively undeveloped previously, it is hard for local decision makers to understand the vast amounts of water needed to support major tourism accommodations. To illustrate, a resort typically requires 350 to 400 gallons of water per room, per day. An 18-hole golf course located in an area without sufficient rainfall to keep it irrigated naturally requires up to a million gallons of water per day. (This is the figure commonly used in the western United States.)

To be competitive, a tourism area must be able to deliver these vast quantities of water conveniently. Inconvenience or inconsistency can very quickly lead to loss of business. For example, if water pressure falls at a facility in the morning when tourists are showering, this will go to the discredit of the hotel and could well hurt its business.

Purity of water is as difficult, in some areas more difficult, to achieve. There are, for example, still many Americans who will not plan on vacations in Mexico because of the horror stories concerning the purity of water. Mexico has, of course, built a substantial tourism industry. However, many attractions in Mexico suffer from unwillingness of tourists to stay in hotels other than those with their own water purification facilities.

Providing quantities of pure water is a costly item in the budget for any area-development program. Alternatives and budgets presented for decision approval can involve the building of dams, development of an entire water basin, extensive well drilling, and networks of aqueducts and pipelines. No matter what other plans are considered, however, it should be remembered that water is the single most critical need in assuring feasibility of tourism development.

POWER

Power is an important convenience item which has become a necessity for virtually any major tourism-development program. Electric power must be plentiful and readily available. To illustrate, a resort hotel will typically consume between 3.25 and 3.75 kilowatt hours of electricity per room, per day.

In setting specifications for power systems, management concern should center around several key factors:

- There should be adequate supplies of power.
- There should be continuity of service. This may well

necessitate setting up supply grids and/or backup generating equipment.

- Peak-load forecasting should be done on the best available information. Systems should be designed to meet these peak-load requirements.

- To the extent possible, the type of power supplied should be compatible with that used in the major market from which tourists will come. Tourists will use a variety of appliances, ranging from hair dryers to electric shavers and possibly even electric toothbrushes. It is far better to generate the correct cycle rate of current than to require all hotels and accommodations in the area to install converters in order to serve their customers.

Over and above these pragmatic considerations, a power system should be based realistically on resources available in an area. The system should use these resources efficiently and with minimum pollution.

Care should also be taken to avoid despoiling natural beauty for power requirements. Consideration should be given to underground transmission where this is feasible. Where above-ground facilities and transmission lines are felt to be necessary, they should be positioned to minimize detraction from the beauty of the area.

COMMUNICATION

Tourists regularly find it necessary to need to communicate with homes or offices which they are getting away from. It is essential that long distance and local telephone, telegraph, and, as appropriate, television services be available. The constraints and requirements discussed in conjunction with power apply broadly to communication services.

Telephone communication is the main concern. As a rule of thumb, hotels and resorts catering to tourists are well advised to plan for one telephone trunk line or outside circuit for each 20 rooms.

SEWAGE AND DRAINAGE

The capacity and quality of sewage and drainage facilities can be a major factor in the success of a tourism program. Tourists simply do not come in large numbers to unclean areas.

In developing nations particularly, sewage and drainage requirements may well be beyond the scope of any planning which has taken place previously. In a resort area, for example, typical requirements for sewage-flow capacity run between 225 and 275 gallons per day for each room. In commercial and industrial areas within a typical tourism destination, drainage requirements generally come to about 1,800 gallons per day for each acre of developed land.

Types of systems and equipment installed in an area will vary with its geographic and geological conditions. Frequently, development of disposal facilities necessary to meet standards imposed by international tourism will also lead to upgrading of services to the local population. Certainly, the possibility of an overall system from which local residents benefit while the area accommodates tourists should be considered.

Sewage and drainage are planning areas requiring technical expertise. Large expenditures are also necessary in many instances. Because it is virtually impossible to develop a major tourism destination without substantial investment in this infrastructure component, careful consideration is essential.

STREETS AND HIGHWAYS

The need for roads to accommodate auto and bus traffic was discussed in the last chapter, which dealt with transportation. However, there are other aspects of street and highway planning which are essential to success of a tourism program. These other considerations deal with the integration of tourism traffic into the normal vehicular and pedestrian flow patterns of an area.

A basic question to be addressed concerns the extent of integration desirable and permissible between normal commercial activities of an area and those associated with tourism business. Some intermixing is, of course, unavoidable. If a tourism destination includes a major city, however, there are important considerations in determining whether and to what degree tourism attractions and accommodations should be isolated. The city itself may provide attraction. If so, consideration may profitably center upon the degree or extent to which isolation and integration are planned for tourism accommodations.

The degree or extent to which tourism and the regular commerce of an area are intermixed will have a heavy impact upon traffic planning. In adding tourists' vehicles to existing traffic loads, resulting volumes may necessitate a network of one-way streets. Additional or different types of traffic signals may be needed. Streets may have to be widened. It may become necessary to condemn land or old buildings to create parking facilities.

Certainly, provisions for parking become an important consideration in thinking about streets and highways. This is particularly true where the commercial outlets in an area represent a tourist attraction. To attract people to shop in specific stores, it has to be convenient for them to get there. There must also be logical pedestrian patterns which bring them to these key locations. The idea is to establish traffic circulation which assures visibility of impulse-marketing areas to prospective customers.

All this should be done, insofar as possible, with minimum impact on the scenic beauty and quaintness of an area. For example, if it becomes necessary to widen or otherwise improve a road normally used by farmers and animal-drawn vehicles, planners will probably want to make some provision for the separation for the slow-moving vehicles and pedestrians from automotive traffic. Similarly, given a choice of routings for highways, planners will probably want to pick locations which make the best view available to tourists.

Finally, of course, roads and streets must be engineered for safety. As appropriate, there should be dividing barriers and guardrails to prevent catastrophic accidents. On high-speed roads, there must be shoulders or turnouts suitable for rest or repair activities, or as view sites.

PARKS AND RECREATION

A park is an area under legislative control for protection of natural resources or the conduct of recreational activities. This takes in a broad spectrum. It is important to identify each potential park area in terms of the resource it is preserving or the recreation it is providing. Planning must then take place to open the area for accessibility for the purpose to which it is dedicated.

This leaves a wide range of planning and operational considerations to be covered. In general, the idea is to strike a balance between attendance and utilization on the one hand and preservation of the visitor experience and enjoyment on the other. This should be done bearing in mind that parks serve both visitors and local residents. Sometimes utilization by visitors and local residents is different. In other instances, the opportunity to provide an atmosphere or activities which encourage visitors and local residents to meet and mix may have value.

In situations where deterioration of natural resources has already taken place, there may have to be a recapturing or conscious construction of scenic elements. An example can be seen in the creation of "green belts" in urban areas. In urban parks particularly, it is important to establish an effective mixture between structures and open space.

In rural areas, there can be a converse problem. In preserving parks and open areas, there has been a tendency, false at least some of the time, to minimize access roads and other facilities. The problem: if an area is really beautiful, people are going to come to it. Unrealistically limited access may serve only to create traffic jams. Yosemite National Park in California is an excellent example of this. Amidst many hundreds of thousands of acres of open space, people are crowded into a densely developed, narrow valley.

The point: parks and recreational facilities should be designed for and adapted to the uses to which they will be put. There should always be some open space, even in the most urbanized of tourism areas.

HEALTH-CARE FACILITIES

People have medical emergencies. All people do. Tourists are no exception. Destination-area planning must recognize this.

The health-care facilities necessary to accommodate tourism will depend largely on anticipated visitor volume, the age groups expected, the types of activities in which they will engage, and local geographic factors. For example, mountain resorts will typically need a number of paraprofessionals trained to deal with persons with heart and respiratory conditions. Ski resorts will need paraprofessionals trained to evacuate accident victims and apply first aid for broken bones. Desert-type resorts will want to train local guides and other personnel to deal with the possible need of supplementary salt by visitors.

Over and above these first-aid-type measures, major medical facilities should be available for use by tourists. This may require a special effort to staff one or more hospitals with personnel who speak the language of the primary market area. Failure to recognize these needs can have drastic results. Recognizing and dealing with them, on the other hand, can be relatively easy and can lead to considerable good will.

EDUCATION SYSTEMS

Building a tourism industry requires people with a wide variety of skills and talents. These requirements are dealt with in a separate chapter on manpower development. It must be recognized, however, that there is a separation between basic education and special training associated with the needs of any one industry.

If local residents are to derive full economic benefits from tourism development, the local education system must bring them to a point of readiness to accept the special training which private or public-sector entities will provide. At very least, local schools should bring students to a point of competence in reading and the basic use of numbers. If students can read fluently and calculate effectively, special-industry training programs can work from there. If schools do not produce a sufficient number of candidates for tourism employment, the local population will lose opportunities or tourism development may actually be stymied for lack of help.

Where a major portion of tourists will come from a primary market area speaking a language other than the local tongue, some bilingual education may be highly desirable, possibly necessary.

LIVING REQUIREMENTS OF EMPLOYEES

If a tourism destination is in an urban area, housing for employees may not be a problem because there may be enough living facilities within commuting distance accessible through use of regular transit service. If an area is remotely located, however, the developer will generally have to provide employee housing.

If employee housing is to be developed, it is usually best that these facilities be separate and distinct from guest accommodations. There should be enough area for both the tourists and employees to go their own respective ways without crowding each other.

The rationale is straightforward: for employees, it is common for workers all over the world to want to get away from their places of employment when they are off duty. For guests, there will typically be a desire to indulge in activities which represent vacation-type luxuries, generally out of economic range and tastes for local employees. Thus, it is best to provide for separate facilities, with space provided for anticipated expansion of each.

In planning for employee housing and recreation, it is generally best to begin by estimating the number of people who will be needed to serve the facilities being constructed. Standards are readily available to determine the number of maids, maintenance personnel, and food and beverage employees needed in different types and sizes of tourism facilities. From this input, an employee census can be projected and facilities planned accordingly. Frequently, it is necessary, on the basis of employee census data, to plan separate living facilities for local managers and executives and for lower-level service employees.

Another employee-facility consideration: if extensive construction is planned, there should be separate provision for temporary quarters to be occupied by construction workers. Such facilities are usually phased out as a project nears completion, then vacated prior to opening of facilities for tourism business.

SECURITY

Security requirements, as in any area, fall into some basic, broad categories: physical, patrol, safety, and surveillance. These topics alone could fill a book. They will not be covered in detail here.

For planning purposes, it is enough to stipulate that the local police force must have qualified people and expertise in these key areas. They must be capable of planning in terms of levels of security and safety, containment of incidents of violence, specifying equipment to implement their programs, and preparing realistic budgets. Should there be problems in meeting these requirements, there are a number of international agencies which can provide help readily and reasonably.

THE TOURISM INFRASTRUCTURE AND THE LOCAL ECONOMY

Though infrastructure development may be mandated by a tourism program, everyone living in the area is affected. In many ways, the impact of infrastructure development improves, or at least modernizes, the lifestyles of local residents. For example, if a superior road is built to serve a tourism destination, the transportation support for the local economy is upgraded as well. If power, potable water, sewage, and telephone systems are created to support tourism facilities, these utilities can have profound impacts upon the lives of local residents, particularly in areas which are emerging economically.

Though infrastructure improvements may be undertaken and justified primarily to facilitate tourism, the potential impacts upon and benefits to local residents should be an integral part of the planning process. To the extent possible, infrastructure improvements should be planned to accrue maximum benefits to local residents while justifying the resources and funding allocated through the economic benefits derived from tourism development.

SYNOPSIS

If a tourism-development program is to succeed, it is necessary to provide life support through a number of infrastructure facilities and services. Collectively, infrastructure elements comprise the system of services and utilities which are essential to the operation of a tourism destination. Included are requirements for both tourists and local residents. Infrastructure projects, described widely as public works, are almost invariably funded and managed by the public sector. A coordinated overall approach to providing infrastructure services is essential. Without coordination, different elements of the infrastructure may infringe upon each other, as happens when a highway obstructs a view of the ocean or restricts access to a beach. Specific areas of infrastructure concern and planning covered in this chapter are water, power, communication, sewage and drainage, streets and highways, parks and recreation, health-care facilities, education systems, and living requirements of employees. Water requirements, in particular, can be staggering. A major tourism resort typically consumes 350 to 400 gallons per room, per day of potable water. An 18-hole golf course in an area without sufficient rainfall for natural irrigation can require up to a million gallons of water daily.

REVIEW QUESTIONS

1. Describe some of the adverse consequences which could result if technicians from separate disciplines were allowed to proceed with infrastructure planning on their own.

2. Explain why water can be the single greatest obstacle to tourism development if advance planning and commitments are inadequate.

3. Describe a situation in which an overall tourism program can benefit from coordination of plans for water, sewage, power, roads, communication services, and parks. Cover the interrelationships between each of these infrastructure elements.

4. Discuss the relationships and degrees of integration or separation appropriate for tourism accommodations and employee housing within a remote-area resort.

14

ACCOMMODATIONS

NEEDS

Accommodations facilities are the places where tourists stop being travelers and become guests. Accommodations facilities are the places where the tourists spend most of their money and time. Thus, the level of guest satisfaction achieved by an area's accommodations facilities will, in large measure, determine the total success of the tourism program.

It becomes highly critical to manage a tourism industry for a matching between the type of accommodations available and the requirements, preferences, and tastes of its prospective tourists. There must be enough accommodations facilities. At the same time, however, an oversupply can become highly embarrassing and expensive. Similarly, there must be the right type or level of accommodations. As appropriate, there must also be a balance between type and level of facility to match the anticipated makeup of the tourism population itself. To succeed to-

174

day, an area will probably need a mixture of accommodations facilities which include different levels of cost and different types and degrees of amenities.

Functional design of tourism accommodations will also have to be tailored to the nature of the area itself. Factors bearing upon design can include local traditions or customs in architecture. Examples of conformance with local design traditions include thatched-roof facilities in Fiji, Tudor architecture in Great Britain, or pagoda-style buildings in Japan. Other functional factors which can impact the design of facilities may include the availability of land area, surrounding natural resources, and climate.

Functional design should also be tailored to the type and length of stay anticipated in accommodations facilities. For example, rooms are apt to be more spacious and more amenities will typically be available at destination facilities than are generally provided in staging areas catering primarily to transient visitors.

Another shaping factor determining accommodations requirements and plans should be competition. Facilities in any given area should be at least as good as those in other destinations striving to sell in the same markets. At the same time, there must be a monitoring of and a planning for internal competition. Internal competition is healthy up to a point. Beyond a given level, however, it can become disastrous to all parties.

In short, there must be a compatibility between tourists and the accommodations which serve them.

CRITERIA FOR SUCCESS

Success is hard to measure for an accommodations facility such as a hotel. Results are realized only after a relatively long cycle of planning, zoning, development, establishment in the marketplace, and revenue production. Financial statements tend to be complex. Standards in the industry, for example, call for the reporting of gross profit figures which represent revenues minus operating costs. Then, separate reporting is done to reflect taxes and amortization of capital investments. Thus, it can be difficult to derive a true earnings figure or to compare it with industry standards because of wide variations in the proportion of capital investment to total cost and variations in interest and tax rates.

For these reasons, the room rate (tariff) and percentage of occupancy has come to be regarded as a standard for reporting and measuring the success of an accommodations property. It is assumed, sometimes erroneously, that management has prorated costs, financing expenses, and operating outlays to arrive at room rate schedules and other charges which will produce profits at a reasonable rate of occupancy. Thus, comparing rates of occupancy between properties and/or areas should reflect relative success.

Broadly, rate of occupancy is a percentage expression of rooms rented as compared with rooms (in some areas, beds) available. Figures are annualized for reporting purposes. In local reports, rates of occupancy are sometimes broken down seasonally or monthly. A typical objective is to structure room rates so that a property operates at breakeven when its rate of occupancy is 50 percent. Thus, an annual rate of occupancy of 70 percent should indicate a healthy level of operating profitability. Average annual occupancy rates ranging anywhere from 60 to 70 percent tend to be regarded as acceptable.

In planning for accommodations, projected visitor volumes should be analyzed carefully, with an eye toward providing enough rooms to house approximately 130 percent of visitors, generating 70 percent occupancy on an annualized basis. This annualized basis, it should be noted, takes into account peak periods when there may actually be a shortage of rooms. By planning for this type of profitable average, it becomes possible for managers to schedule facilities maintenance and employee vacations during relatively slack periods.

Although higher rates of occupancy may sound good, they could cause problems. For example, if a hotel were running at 90 percent occupancy the year round, management should study the feasibility of expansion, since this type of occupancy rate would ultimately lead to undue wear and tear, coupled with inability to keep facilities in first-class condition. It could also be indicative of a situation where a portion of the potential market is turned away, leading these tourists to try other areas, which gain business by default.

TYPES OF FACILITIES

Tourists come from a wide range of economic backgrounds. They have different tastes. They also have widely varying economic means. To build a broadly based industry, it is necessary to develop a range of facilities which appeals to and is affordable by all of the classes or groups of tourists an area plans to attract.

The types and numbers of facilities developed will depend largely upon existing resources and accommodations, analysis of market potential, and upon materials, geography, and financing available.

Tourist accommodation facilities fall into a number of generalized categories, including:

- Hotels (international and standard)
- Motor hotels (international and standard)
- Motels (international and standard)
- Resort hotels (international and standard)
- Condominiums and apartment hotels
- Recreational vehicle parks and campgrounds
- Pensions
- Hostels
- Houseboats or boatels.

Hotels

Normally, hotels are the principal mode of accommodation for a destination. Hotels can also become destinations or attractions on their own. That is, it is possible to have a hotel with sufficient activities and facilities so people simply stay there for their entire vacations, requiring little or no external activities, entertainment, or shopping facilities.

Distinguishing characteristics which set hotels apart from other types of accommodations center around extent or completeness of facilities and services available. In addition to rooms, hotels should have food and beverage service, and a number of convenience services or amenities, such as room service, laundry service, valet service, a sundry shop, and a variety of other shopping or service facilities (auto rental, airline ticketing, tour reservations, and others).

Broadly, hotels tend to be described in terms of two classes or categories — international and standard. The differentiation lies largely in quality and size, with considerable balancing between these factors taking place. For example, a hotel may be large enough to qualify as an international-class facility but it may have guest rooms which are too small or too run down to be considered top quality. Thus, it would tend to be classified as standard. (The same types of criteria are used in classifying motor hotels, motels, and resorts.)

The classification assigned to a hotel can make a difference in its revenues and its profits. By tacit agreement internationally and by legislation in many localities, international-class properties charge higher rates than standard facilities.

Typical qualifications for an international-class hotel might include large guest rooms, well-appointed furnishings, availability of bilingual or multilingual staff, special services for tour and travel planning, barber and beauty shops, spas, quality retail shops, and responsive service to special guest requests and to maintenance requirements.

Standard-class hotels provide many of the same services, but generally with less quality and fewer amenities. Typically, rooms are smaller and furnishings less elegant.

Within these broad classifications, hotels also tend to be described in terms of the functions they perform. For example, there are facilities which are described as convention hotels, transient hotels, or commercial (catering to business travelers) hotels.

Since hotels are used below as a basis for comparison with other types of accommodation facilities, bear in mind that the distinguishing characteristic between types of facilities lie chiefly in the breadth of services offered.

Motor Hotels

A motor hotel is, basically, a hotel with integrated parking facilities. The classic definition of this type of property holds that cars of guests are parked free of charge. This distinction assumes that most guests at conventional hotels arrive by public transportation and that those who drive are charged for parking. As competition has entered individual markets, however, a number of hotels have offered free parking.

In general, motor hotels will tend to be small to medium-size facilities, usually with between 50 and 300 rooms. Beyond this, the space required for parking, and for traffic in and out of the garage or lot, could become a problem.

At very minimum, a motor-hotel property should have integral restaurant and beverage-service facilities. Many motor hotels also have other amenities. These, of course, bear upon whether a motor hotel is placed in the international or standard category.

Motels

Motels are facilities which, in general, focus on providing room accommodations only. They do so at lower prices than hotels or motor hotels. Motels are located chiefly at roadside or heavy-traffic locations, since they are highly dependent upon transients or budget-conscious visitors. Most sales, unless properties are chain-affiliated, are on an impulse-buying basis. Most guests are transients.

This description should not be construed as negative. On the contrary, motels have a definite place in the accommodations portion of most tourism industries. In some areas, they are the backbone of accommodations capabilities. They are especially important for accommodating families who travel by car. They are prevalent in areas characterized by high volumes of visitors who stay for short periods. For example, a high-volume attraction such as Disneyland, with several large hotels and many restaurants in the immediate vicinity, also supports a substantial number of small motels.

Resort Hotels

A resort hotel is dependent upon natural and/or developed amenities which provide recreational attraction to tourists. Typical examples include golf courses, beaches, tennis courts, horseback-riding facilities, ranches, boating, fishing, water skiing, surfing, scuba diving, and other indoor or outdoor recreations popular enough to attract a tourist clientele.

In other words, resort hotels are closely associated with resort areas. There is a tendency to refer to both hotels and the areas in which they are located simply as "resorts." In this book, the term, resort, is used inclusively, referring to an area. Thus, a resort can accommodate multiple hotels or facilities, some of which would be resort hotels. There could, however, also be motor hotels, commerical or convention hotels, or motels in the same area.

A resort hotel, over and above its basic attraction, is also characterized by high quality of services and, usually, relatively high charges. Development density is usually low. Guest rooms are usually large. Many ancillary services are generally included, primarily because of the market it serves and partly because of remoteness of location. These usually take in all of the amenities cited for international-class hotels. In addition, many resort hotels employ social or activity directors who plan group-participation events for guests.

Increasingly, resort hotels are constructing executive conference centers to attract business or professional meetings. Part of the advantage of such facilities lies in their remoteness — people attending conferences have few distractions.

Condominiums and Apartment Hotels

These are accommodations which provide full, apartment-type living facilities — as constrasted with simple guest rooms which lack facilities for cooking and eating within individual units. For the most part, this type of accommodation appeals to families. However, small groups are also frequent users. For example, groups of two or three couples frequently join together to rent an apartment in a condominium.

In addition to these distinctions, there are usually variations in rental plans or guest fees. Costs tend to be lower. Rental is usually by the week or month, rather than on a daily basis.

The chief difference between condominiums and apartment hotels lies in ownership. Apartment hotels, typically, are owned on an equity basis by a single individual or entity. Thus, ownership, management, and operation are integrated.

By contrast, condominums imply separate ownership of individual living units. There may or may not be a separate management and operating function. Increasingly, however, resort or vacation-area condominiums are being operated for tourists or transients. Although there are many variations in the ownership and utilization of condominiums, they tend to fall into two broad categories:

1. Individual families or groups of persons own separate units within a condominium. When the owners are not

using their units, the management of the facility attempts to rent them to visitors. In general, this approach is described as unit ownership with rental-pool agreements. The major distinction is that the owner of each living unit is responsible for purchase and maintenance. If rental incomes do not cover expenses for mortgage payments and maintenance, the individual owners must make up the difference.

2. Many condominiums are sold and/or managed on a timesharing or shared-utilization basis. Under any of a wide variety of plans, individuals contract to use a facility for a limited amount of time each year. Participants can actually own a divided interest in a condominium unit. Or they can have contracts with owners and managers which guarantee availability of a facility for a certain number of weeks each year. Increasingly, these plans involve significant down payments, prepayments, or advances by vacationers. However, such plans usually leave ownership and operating responsibilities in the hands of a management entity, placing limited liability on participating vacationers.

This latter approach enables development-management organizations to derive a substantial portion of the needed capital in advance, under contract from participants. Risks are reduced. Where the primary market for condominium utilization is from another country, this can result in an infusion of hard currency and an enhancement of foreign-exchange position.

To make this type of plan work, however, there must either be a resort or recreational attraction close at hand to hold the interest of guests — as well as to keep them returning for contracted time-slot periods. To illustrate, ski and beach resorts have been prime areas where timesharing condominiums have been offered.

Where a sufficiently popular resort is close at hand, shared use of condominiums serves to assure a certain volume of visitor traffic. Visitors who use these facilities, further, will tend to stay longer than transients or tour groups. Condominium business also tends to be repetitive because of the ownership or contractual ties involved.

Recreational-Vehicle
Parks and Campgrounds

These facilities appeal to families, small groups, or individuals who fit into one of a few special categories:

- Persons may have made a substantial investment in a trailer or motor home. They are, therefore, committed to utilizing their own travel/living facilities on vacations. These vacationers seek the convenience of being able to bring their living facilities with them — as well as the economy of avoiding room rentals.

- There are some persons who enjoy camping experiences. They tend to prefer to spend at least part of each vacation in areas known for natural beauty or wilderness. They, too, carry living facilities with them in the form of camping equipment.

Accommodation facilities catering to this category of visitor are almost always of the low-budget type. There are trailer parks and campgrounds which are quite elaborate, including swimming pools, saunas, and other amenities. However, their rates are still considerably below hotels or motor hotels offering similar luxuries.

Persons seeking this type of accommodation will want to feel that they are getting closer to the culture and the people of the area they visit. These tourists will also tend to be considerably younger than the average visitor to a hotel or motor hotel. However, some relatively affluent families with young children have come to prefer camping-type vacations.

For the host area, recreational-vehicle parks or campgrounds will tend to mean lower levels of cash flow than hotels, motor hotels, or motels designed to accommodate the same numbers of people. This is, however, a potentially important segment of the tourism market.

Pensions

A pension, typically, is an accommodation facility operated by an individual or family in conjunction with the owners' own living quarters. This type of tourist accommodation is particularly popular in continental Europe. The equivalent to this type of facility in the United States is the transient rooming house. In effect, individuals or families accommodate tourists in their own homes. Frequently, pensions also provide family-style meals, either as an option or under an American-plan rate structure.

Since these units tend to be small, they rarely have a major impact on tourism revenues. In relatively congested areas, however, they do hold a potential for handling either overflow or budget-conscious segments of the tourism trade. In some instances, pensions may have a distinctive appeal to the type of tourist who wants to feel the experience of "living among" the indigenous population of the area.

Hostels

These are communal-type facilities typically frequented by youthful travelers who carry their own bedrolls and cooking utensils. They are associated with homes or farms of private families. Rates are extremely reasonable.

For areas which will be catering to a youthful market, this type of accommodation can have some attraction. Its potential drawback is that large numbers of young people traveling on low budgets can deter more affluent tourists from using an area.

Houseboats

Another type of accommodation facility — which is gaining favor from Kashmir, India, to the Sacramento River Valley in California — is the houseboat. In Fort Lauderdale, Florida, a "Flotel," a motel of moored houseboats, has gained immediate tourist acceptance. Though small at this writing, this segment of the accommodations industry may see substantial future growth.

OWNERSHIP AND MANAGEMENT PATTERNS

The wide range of choices in accommodations facilities serves to illustrate one of the challenges associated with developing a "plant" to house an area's visitors. That is, there is a major challenge in deciding just what to build, how much to invest, and what management arrangements to establish.

Basically, a hotel or other accommodations facility is a real-estate property. Similarities center on use of land. But there are also differences. These stem from methods used to determine the value of a hotel or motel. With an office building or apartment house, for example, values tend to center around land and structures. With a hotel, by contrast, valuation is dependent upon business profitability, with land and property values contributing to but not determining worth. Thus, accommodations facilities are capital-intensive investments involving business and market-type risks to a higher degree than conventional real-estate properties. Because of these special characteristics, development and operation of an accommodation facility involves a special blend of investment capital and management talent.

In the majority of situations, management talent becomes the most critical factor. To illustrate, if an international hotel chain undertakes to contract for either a lease or management arrangement for a hotel under development, raising money to build it should be relatively simple. By contrast, a given site and projected facility may have commitments from willing backers but may fail for lack of management talent in its planning and operation.

There is good reason for this type of situation: the day has arrived where a computerized reservation system at the hub of an international network of accommodations outlets may well hold the key to a viable occupancy rate. Under these conditions, cooperative investment plans have abounded. Since international chains of hotels and motor hotels are, increasingly, making their money from operating, rather than building, facilities, they have become less important as investors. This was evidenced in 1975, when, in the United States, Prudential Insurance purchased a 50 percent interest in six Hilton Hotels for $83 million. This arrangement frees Hilton greatly to expand its operations without encumbering capital in ownership. At the same time, these properties, subject to Hilton's skilled management, proved highly attractive for investment portfolios.

Under current money-market and tourism conditions, joint ventures for accommodations investments are becoming commonplace. Typically, at least a substantial part of the capital for accommodations facilities comes from local investors. Many countries have laws which require a stipulated percentage, frequently a majority, of ownership by their own nationals. In some cases, the laws permit local nationals to invest less than the stipulated amount, as long as there is a contract which permits purchase of the designated level of interest within a given time frame. This is attractive to local investors, since they are able to leverage their limited capital by contracting to buy a substantial or controlling interest through reinvestment of operating proceeds.

As attractive as this picture may seem, investors should be aware of the fact that they are taking a disproportionate share of the risk in many hotel and motor hotel situations. If an international chain accepts a management contract, the operating entity is actually contributing little or nothing in the way of cash investment. At the same time, however, the management organization has its reputation and its future at risk each time it goes into a major management contract. It may be true that the management firm can walk away with little or no loss if a property fails. But should this happen too often, this type of deal would quickly become hard to find.

Still another option is for investor-owners to lease a facility to a hotel company. In such situations, the property is identified with the name of the hotel or motor hotel chain and is operated as one of the chain's properties. The operating company undertakes to pay a given rental on a regular basis for use of the facilities. The advantage is that the owner has a high assurance of income return. Conversely, the owners do not share in the profits from the facility in the same degree.

A wide variety of ownership and management patterns is open to the planners and the developers of a tourism program. It becomes important, therefore, to study the alternatives and opportunities and to formulate plans which meet the needs of a destination, within its available resources.

SYNOPSIS

Accommodations facilities are the places where tourists stop being travelers and become guests. These are also the places where tourists spend the majority of their time and money. Therefore, planning for accommodations is critically important to the success of a tourism program. Concerns in planning should include matching facilities to preferences of projected visitors, matching the design and architecture of facilities to the culture and traditions of its area, meeting international competition, and avoiding local competition which can lead to price cutting and destructive overbuilding. Financial reporting practices of the hotel industry are such that accounting statements usually do not provide a valid measure of success. Therefore, a common measure of performance has centered around rates of occupancy — a percentage describing the number of available rooms actually used. Most hotels break even on occupancy rates of approximately 50 percent. Properties are considered profitable if they post year-round averages of 60 to 70 percent occupacny. Types of accommodations facilities described in this chapter are hotels, motor hotels, motels, resort hotels, condominiums and apartment hotels, recreational vehicle parks and campgrounds, pensions, hostels, and houseboat facilities. Ownership and management of accommodations facilities have moved heavily in the direction of cooperative, or joint, ventures. Under a variety of plans gaining popularity, international hotel companies are divesting themselves of ownership in favor of management contracts or leases of properties owned by others. Increasingly, success of a property in international tourism markets depends on the popularity and efficiency of a computerized reservation system in primary tourism markets.

REVIEW QUESTIONS

1. Discuss ways in which a tourism program might suffer from failure to provide accommodations facilities attractive to visitors from its primary market areas.

2. Explain why occupancy rates have emerged as the primary measure of success for accommodations properties.

3. Describe the major distinctions between international and standard-class hotels.

4. Explain the rationale for decisions by a number of international hotel companies to divest themselves of ownership of properties in favor of leasing or management-contract arrangements.

15

SUPPORT INDUSTRIES

HOME-GROWN OPPORTUNITIES

A wide variety of activities, services, and sales outlets comprise what could be called the small-business segment of any tourism industry. There is a tendency to take it for granted that this type of business will materialize wherever tourism develops. Such instincts can be dangerous. Left to their own devices, the small shops, restaurants, sightseeing tours, and other services for or commerce with tourists can quickly become mismanaged and can reflect adversely upon the destination as a whole. Conversely, with comparatively little planning, valuable dividends can be realized in terms of encouraging local entrepreneurs, supporting and building major tourism attractions, imparting pleasant experiences for large numbers of visitors, and increasing length of stay.

Regarded in this way, support industries hold an important key to the success of a tourism destination. One important value lies in providing enough activity potential so that the length of tourist stays will be extended. Obviously, the longer tourists stay, the more they spend. In addition, the longer the stay which can be justified, the wider the destination's potential market range will be, since transportation costs are amortized over longer periods. Thus, if a group of shops or a museum builds sufficient reputation so that tourists routinely block a half day or a full day for browsing there, this contributes to the destination's overall success.

An excellent example can be seen in San Francisco. Fisherman's Wharf, with its series of restaurants and souvenir shops, has long been regarded as a must for at least one evening by most visitors to San Francisco. Recently, two major groups of handicraft, art, fashion, and home furnishing shops have been added to this area — at Ghiradelli Square and The Cannery. With the addition of these facilities, which are comprised of classic-type support industries, many tourists are now spending an entire day rather than just one evening, in the same area of the city.

Demonstrating how public-sector planning can accomplish the same thing, consider the museum of archeology in Mexico City. This attraction routinely occupies a half day to a full day of time for many tourists, extending their interest level and stay in Mexico City. The same, in general, applies to the many public markets in which government agencies in Mexico rent stalls to local artisans or retailers. Other examples can be seen in such long-established areas as the Soho in London or the Left Bank in Paris.

NATURE OF SUPPORT INDUSTRIES

As indicated by the foregoing examples, support industries can be both public and private in nature. Economically, a major characteristic is that they are highly fragmented — consisting of a seemingly infinite number of highly individual parts. Collectively, however, these small enterprises constitute a major segment of the tourism business as a whole.

Further, their importance is magnified by the fact that they are highly visible to the tourists themselves and, because of this, can have a major impact on the tourist experience. Thus, the total group of support industries can serve either to enhance or detract from the major investments in site development and facilities of other segments of the tourism industry.

Potential problems and dangers lie in the fact that this major force for either positive or negative impact seems to be beyond the reasonable reach of management methods applied on a larger scale by the major corporate or governmental entities responsible for the primary undertakings of the tourism industry.

A "typical" support-type business does not lend itself well to corporate or governmental-type management because of its basic characteristics. Usually, this segment of the industry is made up of a lot of small businesses, although governments frequently operate this type of activity. Each individual business, in turn, tends to be labor intensive but to require comparatively little capital.

Consider, for example, a handicraft shop. An individual may be able to open a shop or stall to sell handicrafts with a total capital of a few hundred or a few thousand dollars. The key ingredients are the long hours and hard work necessary. Another essential is entrepreneurial commitment. Virtually all business transacted by the handicraft shop, for example, is in cash. If the owner is not running the facility, there could be massive problems in inventory and cash control. Further, only an involved entrepreneur can profitably engage in the bargaining and price adjustments necessary in this type of small business in many tourism areas.

On the one hand, then, the nature of support industries is that they provide opportunities for local entrepreneurs to build profitable ventures with relatively small individual investments. In many areas, this segment of the tourism industry makes a major contribution in meeting aspirations of emerging middle class groups.

Despite small size and fragmented ownership, some measure of control and direction is essential. The entire tourism destination can be hurt if a reputation emerges for overcharging, short changing, or selling shoddy merchandise. Similarly, if individual shops are unkempt or inaccessible, this segment of the tourism industry may not develop to its full potential.

Thus, planning for support industries can benefit the entire tourism program. It can, for instance, pay excellent dividends to designate specific areas for support-industry types of activities. The example of Fisherman's Wharf and other close by attractions, Ghiradelli Square and The Cannery, illustrates this practice. The public sector has cooperated by providing favorable zoning, making parking facilities available, and other planning-type cooperation. This, in turn, has made it attractive for private-sector investors to acquire the facilities and make them available to large numbers of individual and small-business enterprises.

Public-sector entities also become involved in this type of activity. For example, many port or marina areas use public lands and public facilities leased to private businesses. The important element of control is that cooperation is planned and executed by a large public or private-sector entity which owns and controls land or facilities. The act of creating facilities and leasing them to small business provides the control necessary for assurance of compatibility with the tourism industry as a whole while still creating opportunities for smaller-scale entrepreneurs.

TYPES OF SUPPORT BUSINESSES

Broadly, support industries, within the present context, encompass all services, goods, or activities required by tourists which do not fall within the previously described areas of infrastructure, transportation, or accommodations. Types of businesses or services covered include:

- Local or day tours
- Retail shops selling locally produced goods
- Retail shops selling international goods at reduced prices (in duty-free or tax-free areas)
- Art galleries
- Restaurants
- Night clubs or live-entertainment theaters
- Museums or special exhibit facilities, both public and private
- Recreation facilities
- Recreation services where facilities are part of the infrastructure (boat or scuba equipment rental at beaches, stable or horse-rental services, guide services at public parks, etc.)
- Motion picture theaters
- Handicraft production facilities or studios
- Golf courses or other participation sports activities
- Spectator sports
- Festivals

- Regularly staged festive events based on local customs
- Laundries
- Pharmacies
- Maps, guide books, brochures, post cards, and directories
- Gasoline filling stations
- Book stores, department stores, food stores, or other retail outlets of interest to tourists planning extended stays or with an interest in local customs or lifestyles
- Gaming.

PLANNING AND MANAGEMENT CHALLENGES

Since support industries are necessary for tourism success, they should receive the same type and caliber of planning and management direction as the rest of the development program. Specific areas of planning and management concern include:

1. Identifying opportunity areas
2. Level of service
3. Facilities planning and standards
4. Increasing tourism activity and length of stay
5. Setting standards for pricing, quality, and business ethics
6. Providing profit opportunities for local entrepreneurs.

Identifying Opportunity Areas

Support-industry opportunities fall into two broad areas:

1. Impulse or entertainment purchases which are pleasure-related
2. Staple items or requirements which are subsistence-related.

Capabilities and facilities in both areas are mandatory. These capabilities and facilities should be integrated for convenience, and for profitability, within tourism traffic and circulation patterns. Suppose, for example, an area is dedicated largely to fashion and jewelry shops. Shoppers lingering in this neighborhood will require snack bars, possibly a place to purchase aspirins, or other requirements or amenities.

Identification of such opportunities and requirements should stem from the initial, overall tourism market studies and forecasts. As described earlier, part of the basic planning process involves an inventorying of attributes and prospective attractions. Allocation of land, facilities, traffic circulation, and other elements of a tourism industry should then provide for facilities and services which capitalize on these attributes.

The previously cited situation of Fisherman's Wharf offers a good illustration. Historically, the wharf area from which the fishing fleet operated was a major point of interest in San Francisco. As the city expanded its commercial facilities into this area, there was actual danger at one time that the fishing fleet would move elsewhere to get away from rising costs and other inconveniences. The city then moved in to subsidize some of the facilities to keep them viably priced for the fishing fleet operators. City-owned or controlled facilities were then made available for conversion to restaurants and shops. Other areas were zoned attractively for conversion to tourism-support facilities. Thus, it became attractive and profitable to convert former fish canneries or chocolate factories for tourist use.

Another type of example can be seen in the building of clothing and tailoring activities in Hong Kong. Because Hong Kong is a duty-free port, import of top-quality fabrics from all over the world became highly attractive. To build upon this potential opportunity, local business people were encouraged to develop skills and train residents as tailors. Ultimately, a major business with visiting tourists and through overseas mail sales evolved.

The building of artisans' markets by the Mexican government is another example. This type of facility affects large segments of the population, since actual manufacturing or production of handicraft items is done in rural areas. Thousands of independent merchants build business enterprises through the distribution and sale of these items.

Level of Service

Having identified opportunities, planners should then recognize that it is possible to have too much — or too little — of a good thing. Undersupply fails to stimulate sufficient demand to build a market. Oversupply depresses profitability.

Within these broad ranges, planning should take place for the availability of materials or items based on circulation and visitation patterns — within spending projections. As part of the tourism market-planning study, projections should be made about the number of visitors who can be expected and their areas of origin. Based on these data, reliable assumptions can be made about discretionary or disposable funds available to these visitors. There are many studies, made all over the world, projecting levels of spending which can be expected from visitors for different kinds of items — souvenirs, clothing, handicraft specialties, jewelry, silver, gold, and so on. Therefore, it becomes necessary, once local opportunities are identified, to establish a pattern for delivering appropriate items to tourists and for deriving projected incomes for entrepreneurs.

This should be done on an area or regional basis. In an area established for browsing or shopping, it makes sense to cluster facilities according to type or compatibility of merchandise or services involved. The example of a snack shop in a shopping area represents one type of mixture requirement. Also, for example, an area selling women's dresses should also have stores nearby selling handbags and shoes.

There should also be a mixture in types of offerings. For example, if all of the women's dress shops in a given tourism area were in a single neighborhood, a phenomenon known as visual overkill could set in. Shoppers would simply be overwhelmed.

Facilities also have to be related to each other. For example, restaurants featuring gourmet dinners should be in proximity to the highest-priced hotels in the area. The same would be true for nightclubs.

This is perhaps the most painstaking and detailed part of facilities planning associated with successful tourism. It can be tedious. It will always be highly detailed. However, failure to accord sufficient attention to mix, location, and interrelationships between support industries can have adverse effects.

Facilities Planning and Standards

Effective support facilities result from controlled approaches to the establishing of standards and operating conditions. Two primary techniques can be exercised to achieve this control:

1. Zoning and operating regulations enforced by law

    2. Ownership or control exercised through leasing of
       facilities to individual entrepreneurs.

The two methods are not mutually exclusive. Best results may well be derived from a combination of both approaches. Actually, the ability to own or control a large facility and lease portions of the area to individual entrepreneurs appears to have produced the best results. Through leasing control, management can exercise restrictions or direction over the types of businesses established, their density, and their appearance.

One effective approach to setting facilities plans and standards is to establish theme areas or villages in which all facilities conform to a uniform pattern or type of decor. An example of achievement of this type of image and business pattern through zoning controls over privately-owned facilities can be seen in Monterey and Carmel, California. These cities are highly successful as tourism attractions, largely because of their scenic, climatic, and waterfront locations. These natural attributes have been used to advantage through zoning controls or restrictions which require that the historic and scenic advantages of such established areas as Cannery Row be kept intact and developed through plans which do not destroy original appearances or decor.

The same type of objective can be accomplished when a theme area or village is built from scratch. Greenfield Village, Michigan, and Old Sturbridge, Massachusetts, are examples. At Old Sturbridge, a village was built from the ground up following "typical" plans and patterns of the Revolutionary era. This work was undertaken by a single, private developer with government support and encouragement. Restaurants, shops, a grist mill, and other attractions were all installed on a planned basis, making for an integrated, pleasant, overall tourist experience. Plans, however, included leasing of facilities to independent local entrepreneurs.

No matter what approach is taken, experience with tourism facilities all over the world has tended to identify some common denominators which should be observed. These include:

- Height restrictions for buildings
- Developmental density
- Requirements for green belts or walkways
- Signing codes or restrictions
- Parking facilities and requirements

- Scenic exposure, particularly for facilities where visitors will spend considerable amounts of time (such as restaurants)
- Restrictions covering display-window size and extent of exposure
- Overall image of the area
- Architectural styles
- Provisions for plan approvals by government bodies or committees of local business people.

Increasing Tourism Activity And Length of Stay

A successful group or enclave of support businesses can comprise an attraction which increases length of stay and revenue from tourism. When this is done, there is a leveraging effect as swarms of small entrepreneurs add the weight of their investments to the overall tourism effort. Coordination is the key. Through careful planning, groups of individual entrepreneurs who could not have a major impact on the tourism industry by themselves can, in fact, have an important effect collectively. The cumulative effect of these efforts can result in a longer, more enjoyable stay for the tourist and increased revenues in all sectors of the destination.

Setting Standards For Pricing, Quality, and Business Ethics

Small businessmen in particular tend to take a short-range look at business transactions with tourists. The tourist who buys something today, it is reasoned, will be gone tomorrow. Why not take some extra profit?

The answer, obviously, is that word gets around. A tourist who is satisfied will tell the folks back home. Everyone in the tourism area can benefit. A careful mixture of education, regulation, and enforcement tends to be necessary. Individual entrepreneurs must realize, first, that it is to their own advantage to deal fairly and equitably with tourists.

In some areas, it may be necessary to help educate individual entrepreneurs in the principles of business management. A restaurant which is overproducing meals may, for example, be tempted to raise prices to cope with its waste factor. This simply compounds the overproduction problem as business falls off. Similarly, unrealistically inflated inventory levels among shopkeepers can lead to price wars which cause failures, reduce confidence in the pricing of other products, or both. Part of the answer, obviously, lies in helping small local businessmen to learn to manage for bottom-line results.

In addition, however, the local government should set up standards and provide mechanisms for inspection, enforcement, and customer recourse with complaints. Persons entering into business ventures in the area should be advised, from the beginning, what these standards and operating conditions are and why they exist.

Persons assigned to monitor and enforce these standards should have guidelines to help in their efforts. These guidelines should include enough knowlegeability about items or services to judge quality. Pricing in relation to quality should also be monitored through some system of guidelines. For example, it can be highly disappointing for a tourist to make a "duty-free" purchase in the departure lounge of an airport only to find the same item available at lower cost in a local supermarket or variety store on returning home. Such ill-considered pricing policies lead tourists to feel that they have been treated unfairly. A single experience of this type can reflect badly upon an otherwise-pleasant vacation.

Providing Proper Opportunities for Local Entrepreneurs

In addition to monitoring the quality of items or services sold and their prices, care should also be exercised to encourage quality local people to get into this kind of business. To do this, it is necessary to structure situations which provide a high level of assurance that individual entrepreneurs will realize reasonable returns on their investments and efforts. This can be accomplished through control of leasing arrangements, through examination and reasonable structuring of taxes, and through monitoring of infrastructure services upon which local business organizations are dependent.

Ideally, small business people within an area should have someplace to turn within the government or private sector for

assistance in evaluating the efficiency and profitability of individual businesses. These resources can include private consulting, government counseling, or possibly a combination of efforts. The point: if local, individual entrepreneurs do not realize
a return, this too can hurt the tourism industry.

Within any given tourism area, support industries will be the
hardest to control and the most fragmented segment. Care
should be taken to avoid a throwing up of hands and letting this
important segment of the industry drift without direction or control. Without adequate attention, support industries can become
an Achilles heel. Carefully managed and supported, on the other
hand, they can be part of a bright overall picture.

SYNOPSIS

Support industries, as described in this chapter, include all of
the ancillary services required or desired by tourists to enhance
their visitation experience in a destination. Covered are a range
of enterprises encompassing local tours, retail shops,
restaurants, entertainment facilities, museums, recreation
facilities other than major theme parks, motion picture theaters,
festivals, automotive service stations, and others. To a large
degree, support industries are part of the private sector and are
operated by small, independent entrepreneurs. Despite the in-
dependence and widespread ownership characterized by this
sector of a tourism program, it is still necessary to plan for and
apply management controls to add to the positive image of
tourism while avoiding negative impact which can result from inadequate services, poor quality, overcharging, or other abuses. A
six-part technique for applying these necessary controls is outlined. This includes: identifying opportunity areas; determining
appropriate levels of service; establishing plans and operating
standards; creating levels of activity and interest which will increase the length of tourism stays; setting and monitoring standards for pricing, quality, and business ethics, and assuring profit
opportunities for local entrepreneurs.

REVIEW QUESTIONS

1. Describe the negative impact which a tourism destination could suffer if support industries were permitted to go completely uncontrolled.

2. Describe the potential benefits to a tourism destination for planning and monitoring the operation of support industries.

3. Explain why support businesses and services are generally owned and operated by local entrepreneurs.

4. Describe some of the economic benefits which can accrue to an area from programs to encourage independent persons to establish tourism-support-type businesses.

5. Describe the steps appropriate to establishing an effective balance in support-industry services and facilities within a tourism destination. Include consideration of the factors of undersupply and visual overkill.

16

DEVELOPING HUMAN RESOURCES

HUMAN EQUATIONS FOR TOURISM SUCCESS

Tourism is a business of human relations. None of the vast investments and facilities associated with tourism development can produce a return unless, in the final analysis, people please people. Visiting people must be pleased with what they see and experience in their dealings with local people.

From the tourism investor's viewpoint, this can be an area of great exposure and/or risk. It is literally possible to build a multi-million-dollar tourism plant and then to be forced — through shortsightedness or planning failures — to put this business into the hands of undereducated, undertrained, underqualified persons with negative attitudes. Putting it another way, a people failure holds the potential for disaster.

Tourism as an industry is not only people oriented, it is also people dependent. A pleasant experience for visitors is one facet, or factor, which must be present for tourism success.

199

Another important factor lies in the balancing of the skills and the personalities of the employees of a tourism industry. To achieve this balance, separate evaluations, supported by appropriate training and development, are necessary in two specific areas of employee qualification:

- Attitudinal
- Technical.

Each of these qualification areas has its own requirements and personnel-development challenges.

ATTITUDINAL QUALIFICATIONS AND REQUIREMENTS

Attitudinal qualifications and requirements for tourism-industry personnel fall into several important categories:

- Pride
- Patience
- Flexibility
- Judgment
- Adaptability.

Pride

Pride has many dimensions — heritage, culture, nationalism, individual progress, satisfaction from a job well done, and a sense of security and identity. These are the kinds of traits about which it is said: people are born with them; either they have them or they don't. This is true up to a point. Certainly, considerable portions of all of these types of pride derive from heredity or tradition. But there is also a danger of having these natural traits broken down or subdued in a service-type environment.

How does a poor person show pride while functioning as a busboy, waiter, or a maid serving wealthy persons from foreign lands who have little or no understanding and appreciation of local culture and customs?

Answer: feeling and demonstrating pride differs with environmental situations. It is possible for persons to demonstrate exceptional pride in dealing with peers, family, or sympathetic superiors while the component traits which add up to a display of pride break down in a service-oriented environment. One way to retain the valued pride within the bearing of employees is through education and training which stress the differences between service occupations, which can be performed with pride, and conditions of servitude, which are debasing.

No matter how lowly a position a person must hold, it is a real asset for the tourism industry, for the individual employer, and for the host area if an appreciation has been developed for the opportunities which stem from sharing the environment and its resources with foreign or out-of-area visitors. Conversely, a loss of pride can lead to surliness which, almost inevitably, contributes to a degrading of service and a loss of tourism business. Thus, the pride which makes for friendliness and openness in dealing with tourists is worth looking for in individuals hired. This trait is also worth cultivating and maintaining through recognition and praise for satisfactory performance once the individual has been employed and trained.

Patience

Tourists, individually and collectively, can be trying people for persons whose job it is to serve them. It is necessary for employees who deal with tourists to have higher-than-average traits of compassion, understanding, and patience.

The requirement of patience among tourism employees is easily demonstrated. A tourist arrives in a destination area after a long, arduous trip. Frequently, deplaning tourists are either too hot, too cold, burdened down with too much carry-on luggage, and generally irrascible. And that's only a beginning. Given this entry-point attitude, tourists then endure a long line at immigration, seemingly unreasonable waits for luggage, and customs inspections. After that, they deal with porters, taxi drivers, and other attendants who may be foreign to them. Many of these dealings involve strange places and strange currencies.

Clearly, success requires patience on the part of service personnel. A personnel training and development program which builds in understanding of these kinds of factors contributes substantially to the prospective success of any tourism venture.

Flexibility

Tourists the world over are notorious for changing their minds. This, too, is understandable. Most of them are coming to a strange place. They are discovering new interests and attractions. They are apt to be changeable in determining what they want to do and where they want to go.

Faced with this kind of characteristic in their clientele, tourism-industry employees require a knack — both natural and developed — for changing plans or adapting to unexpected requests with understanding and willingness.

Judgment

It is impossible to cover every job requirement and contingency in a training program or employee operating manual. This is particularly true in the performance of people-related jobs like those associated with tourism. Consider a relatively typical situation: a tourist on a trip with a local guide or chauffeur decides to make a detour to visit another attraction either in addition to or instead of the one originally designated. One type of problem can arise if the driver advises his client that he cannot change courses or destinations without approval. Still another type of problem can arise if a tourist, who thinks the side trip is routine, discovers at the end of the day that charges have been doubled.

Clearly, it takes judgment on the part of the individual employee to know what to do and how to deal with situations, particularly where costs which may be unexpected are to be incurred by tourists. Individual employees, particularly those who are new to tourism jobs, may not be prepared for or have the judgment to handle such situations. To the extent possible, contingencies should be foreseen and employees trained for them. Beyond that, employees should be grounded through their training — perhaps with role-play techniques — to cope with judgmental demands and/or situations.

Adaptability

Although frequently overlooked, one of the essentials of any tourism employee is that he or she be able to get along with, cooperate, live, and work in harmony with fellow workers. Tourism service, when carried out effectively, is a team effort. Employees of tourism establishments should be team players. Frictions between employees become rapidly apparent to guests. The effect can be highly negative in terms of both impact on guests and disruptions of operations. Therefore, in screening and testing prospective employees, steps should be taken to identify and employ persons who are amenable to working with others to meet common objectives and goals.

In suggesting that prospective employees be recruited and screened in connection with these attitudinal traits, it is assumed that the prospective destination has an abundance of labor. This is almost prerequisite. Labor-short areas would be advised to consider this assumption as part of their planning.

Given an ample supply of labor, it becomes important to present a tourism-development program to the local populace as an opportunity for advancement, growth, and gainful employment. This image should be integrated into the tourism-development program.

TECHNICAL QUALIFICATIONS AND REQUIREMENTS

Individuals or groups within the labor force serving a tourism industry need to acquire and/or develop expertise in specific, specialized operational areas, including:

- Facilities operation
- Equipment operation and maintenance
- Financial management
- Food and beverage production and services
- Personnel management
- Business organization and management
- Systems analysis and design.

Facilities Operation

Operation and maintenance of tourism facilities require a broad spectrum of technical specialties ranging from the relatively simple to the highly technical. Training requirements vary accordingly. For example, maids hired from remote, rural areas may never have encountered box springs, mattresses, or clean sheets and pillows. This represents one kind of challenge in training and supervision.

On the other end of the spectrum, tourism facilities need experienced, reliable plumbers, electricians, refrigeration engineers, and power specialists.

These and other technical skills may or may not be readily available in any given area. Certainly, a major surge in tourism development will increase demands and pose human-resources challenges.

Equipment Operation and Maintenance

These skills may resemble and be related to those associated with facilities operation. But they may also be different. A tourism industry, for example, will need typists, adding machine operators, copying machine operators, bookkeeping machine operators, possibly computer operators, and other types of people who may be in short supply, even in relatively developed areas.

Financial Management

At least some of the persons in tourism jobs will be expected to handle more money than they have encountered previously. Special skills and disciplines must be developed. People must understand systems for handling and controlling money. People must understand the rudiments of cashiering, banking transactions, and overall financial management and control. In most developing areas, at least some special recruiting, screening, and training will be necessary. Requirements can be especially critical if the destination will have casino gaming.

Food and Beverage Production and Service

Almost any developing tourism destination will have to expand and enhance its food production, processing, distribution, and handling capabilities. This can involve special procedures in farming, processing, refrigerated distribution, slaughtering, dressing, storage, and delivery. In addition, within individual hotels and restaurants, comparatively large numbers of chefs, cooks, food-preparation personnel, and food servers must be trained.

From a management standpoint, the challenge lies in identifying, achieving, and maintaining the most appropriate cuisine for the tourist clientele which can be implemented with the skills available. This does *not* mean that every tourism area must develop gourmet food capabilities. Quite to the contrary, in some areas this might not be appropriate. For example, if it becomes necessary to run extensive food and beverage operations using personnel with only limited training and experience, it may be better to develop and stress a selection of local dishes prepared to the highest possible quality rather than attempt to install continental menus and service.

Special challenges will be involved in situations where menu items or beverages are strange to the tastes and customs of local employees. In such cases, it is necessary to train service personnel concerning the tastes and standards of their guests.

Personnel Management

Tourism enterprises may well be larger than most existing organizational entities in their area. The concept of a separate personnel-management function may be new or different within the local economy.

In tourism enterprises, where 35 to 40 percent of revenues go into labor costs, personnel management can become a major undertaking. In many situations, it is necessary to start almost from scratch in developing people who understand the basics of personnel management and who also have a workable knowledge of the specialties and skills they recruit.

Business Organization and Management

The same requirements, in essence, emerge in other organizational and management areas. Skills and experience in data processing, purchasing, or accounting may be scarce in the area. The challenge lies in producing a cadre of middle managers who develop a level of both practical and theoretical knowledge which enables them to meet the dual challenges of ongoing management of existing operations while adapting more sophisticated techniques evolved elsewhere to local advantage.

Systems Analysis and Design

These are skills frequently associated with computer systems. But they are also general requirements in relatively large organizations. Systems, as the term is used within the tourism industry, generally encompass combinations of people, procedures, equipment, and materials working in coordination to accomplish predetermined results. Achieving these results may involve automated equipment or computers, strictly manual procedures, or a combination of both. Certainly qualified systems people will have to be on the scene before major hotel or airport construction projects begin. In many cases, special recruitment of foreign nationals and training programs are necessary to achieve the required degree of knowledge and experience.

An understanding of these balanced requirements is an essential starting point for a program aimed at developing and providing the human resources essential to successful tourism. Given this understanding, a tourism-development program can proceed with the planning and implementation steps described in the remainder of this chapter.

STAFF PLANNING

Staff planning is a process involving systems-analysis techniques. It results in a projection of the kinds and numbers of people who will be needed by all segments of the tourism industry. A typical objective is to orient a staff-planning study to create as many jobs as possible — at satisfactory wage levels — for local citizens. Typical steps associated with a staff-planning study include:

- Job analysis
- Setting requirements and standards
- Preparing job descriptions
- Preparing job specifications
- Preparing staff forecasts.

Although the descriptions which follow trace staff planning at an overall, area level, the same procedures should be adapted and applied to individual hotels, resorts, or other major facilities.

Job Analysis

For each major entity within a tourism industry, a typical approach to a staff-planning study begins by listing all functions to be performed. Broadly, functions are segregated at the outset between those involving guest contact and those regarded as "back of the house" jobs.

Using data from the market study and forecast, the staff-planning analysts estimate the volume of work within each category. These volume figures, in turn, make it possible to break down the isolated functions into separate jobs.

At this initial stage, the job breakdowns are preliminary in nature. To illustrate, a forecast on the number of meals to be served in a given restaurant will enable an experienced analyst to determine whether waiters or waitresses should clear their own tables or whether busboys should be employed.

Similarly, forecasts for a hotel will make it possible to project whether separate bellhops and doormen will be needed, whether bellhops will handle food orders for room service or whether separate waiters will be employed, and so on. The end result of this phase of a staff-planning study is a preliminary list of job titles and an indication of the type and level of people who will be needed to fill these positions.

Setting Requirements and Standards

During this step, the preliminary descriptions of jobs are refined further to incorporate the general duties and levels of skills which will be required. For example, a job-analysis forecast may indicate that chefs and cooks will be necessary. At this point, determinations are made on whether gourmet chefs are to be employed, whether experienced cooks will be needed, or whether short-order cooks can support given facilities.

The same would be true, for example, for the front-desk operation of a hotel. As part of job analysis, separate desk clerk and cashiering functions may be identified for a planned hotel. At this point, a determination is made on whether the same person can do both jobs or whether separate departmental positions will be established. Further, during this phase, breakdowns begin in the number of shifts and the functions to be performed on each. For example, cashiers may be employed on two shifts but not a third. A third-shift desk clerk may double as a night auditor.

Within each of the categories identified, the level of experience or skill of individual employees and their mix as a staff are forecast.

Preparing Job Descriptions

After requirements and standards have been specified, the next step is to prepare descriptions which serve as a basis for recruiting personnel, either locally or on the international market. These are standard job descriptions of the type which can be circulated to prospective employees, employment agencies, or used as a basis for advertising.

Preparing Job Specifications

To supplement job descriptions, job documentation is carried to the "doing" level. That is, actual job-performance manuals are written. Descriptions get down to the individual tasks and subtasks to be performed within individual jobs. For example, job specifications for cashiers would include separate task descriptions for the posting of room charges, the posting of charges for ancillary services, a daily totaling of room bills, checkout procedures, and so on. Documents of this type are also known as operations manuals within some organizations or industries.

Preparing Staff Forecasts

Given the documentation and volume forecasts which have gone into staff planning, the final step lies in determining how many people will be needed, in which departments, on what shifts. In effect, this task within the staff-planning study produces an employee roster which is set and ready for recruiting and employment. Included in the outputs of this final task are schedules on when individuals should be employed, how fast the staff should be expanded, and so on.

LOCAL SKILLS INVENTORY

The next step in human-resources planning is to identify employee sources. Most tourism project managers make it a practice to fill as many projected jobs as possible with local people. This is done either by utilizing existing resources or by establishing plans to develop the necessary skills within existing schedules. This generally involves coordination with the labor department or similar arm of local government. Frequently involved also are surveys of local schools, technical colleges, or universities.

The effort produces an inventory of available and projected skills, taken in much the same way as any other inventory of natural resources. To accomplish this survey on a constructive basis, criteria should be stated in terms which are locally meaningful. For example, it might have little or no meaning to persons conducting this survey to indicate that so many bellhops will be required. It would, however, be highly meaningful to indicate a need for persons with a high-school education, neat appearance, physical fitness, and, to the extent possible, some appropriate bilingual capabilities.

Similarly, rather than indicating that cashiers are needed, it is more effective to indicate educational entry points and training-time requirements. Thus, persons documenting this skills inventory might search for persons with high-school diplomas, competence in computational skills, proven honesty, bondability, bilingual capabilities as appropriate, and any other stated prerequisites.

It could then be stipulated that these persons would have to be hired under a schedule to allow 30 days for training prior to the opening of the facilities where they will be employed. It would then become necessary, of course, to be sure that a conveniently located training facility was available and that class schedules were compatible with training-completion requirements.

The end result of this activity is a forecast covering the numbers and types of people who can be hired locally.

DETERMINING NEEDS FOR IMPORTED SKILLS

This activity is frequently a necessary, though unpopular and potentially controversial, part of human-resources planning. Far from the least of the challenges involved can be the considerable political, bureaucratic, and legislative obstacles to acquisition of needed, qualified personnel. It may be necessary, for example, to waive or alter existing immigration laws or to issue special permits for foreigners with needed skills.

This is why the approach suggested calls for a review of requirements for imported skills after a local skills inventory has been taken and matched with projected human-resources needs. If these earlier activities are carried out effectively, they will produce convincing evidence of actual, minimal requirements for skills which cannot be met from the local area, even with projected investments in education and training. This irreducible minimum of requirements for foreign employees then becomes the request for variances in immigration and residence regulations.

As part of this activity, it is usually sound policy to incorporate a statement of objectives and plans for the training of local personnel to acquire these short-supply skills and experience. Typically, imported skills will consist primarily of high-technology or top-managment positions. The necessary permits are usually requested for limited periods. These requests become even more logical when it can be shown that foreign managers will devote specified, substantial amounts of time to the training of local personnel who will ultimately assume advanced positions.

A word of caution: special care should be taken to be realistic in presenting requests for immigration and residence permits for foreigners. Typically, the planning group will get one opportunity to have a series of special permits issued. Coming back at a later date for additional permits risks unnecessary friction.

THE HUMAN-RESOURCES (MANPOWER) PLAN

Given successful completion of the activities described thus far, an overall human-resources (or manpower) plan can now be put together for the entire tourism program. This is part of a cumulative process. After personnel needs and sources have been determined, the next step is to add a financial dimension, which, in turn, becomes part of the cost presentations incorporated in the overall master plan.

It is necessary to perform this planning step before recruiting begins because earnings and benefits guidelines for employees must now be developed. Without such guidelines, there can be chaos in the hiring and training of people because there would be no basis for establishing wages or working conditions.

When completed, the human-resources plan serves as a basis for implementing a program of recruiting and developing employees. Implementation steps within an overall human-resources program are discussed in the sections which follow.

RECRUITING

Different approaches and types of emphasis are advisable for foreign and domestic recruiting. In foreign recruiting, the emphasis is heavily on quality. The idea is to find the best, most experienced people available commensurate with employment conditions — and then to be sure that they understand the transitional nature of employment and are willing to help build the skills of local personnel.

Domestically, the emphasis has to be on fairness. The idea is to convince the local populace that the program is designed specifically to give as many people as possible a chance to improve their situations.

Structured channels are available for recruiting on the international scene. These include established personnel agencies specializing in accommodations-industry placements, respected business publications which carry classified advertising, and a number of colleges and universities which maintain placement services for graduates.

Domestically, recruiting methods may vary. In some locales, it is desirable and/or necessary to work through existing unions or labor organizations. In other situations, political parties must become involved. At very least, it is desirable to involve an area's educators. In domestic recruiting, the basic principle is that activities should be as broad as possible and offer opportunities to as many persons as possible.

CAREER-PATH PLANNING

The more opportunity a tourism program provides, the greater its acceptance and success are apt to be. Therefore, an important aspect of human-resources management lies in identifying and highlighting growth opportunities for persons who start their careers in tourist-industry occupations at beginning, or entry levels.

This phase of planning should include programs of apprenticeship or internship for students, recent graduates, and also for persons seeking purely vocational careers.

These program outlines should identify continuing-education opportunities and requirements. Some of these may be implemented in conjunction with local technical colleges or universities. Others may be associated with special vocational schools or even private institutions. In addition, individual government or corporate entities may establish training institutes to help develop personnel.

The need in describing careers is for complete honesty. It is just as important to identify jobs without promotion potential as it is to stipulate growth opportunities and upward pathing.

This discussion should not be construed as recommending any rigidity in career pathing or personal development. The basic idea is to create an inventory of opportunities. The paths designated, however, should have as many branches as possible. Thus, in outlining internship or apprenticeship programs, it is sound practice to identify decision points or alternatives available to individuals seeking to better themselves.

EDUCATION

A distinction should be made between education and training in human-resources development. Education includes the intellectual and professional development of a person without concern for specific jobs or responsibilities. Thus, education would involve such goals as literacy, command of foreign languages, knowledge of the history and customs of the country, basic computational skills, and so on.

Once a decision has been reached to develop a significant tourism industry, it is valuable to communicate the desirable traits of its employees to all levels within the educational system. These days, education in economics is beginning at elementary grades. Thus, it would be very much in order for tourism officials to work with curriculum coordinators in introducing concepts about cultural interchange and economic advantages of tourism at all levels within a local education system.

In secondary and higher-education institutions, vocational and management training enter the picture. Vocational-education curricula in hospitality and tourism have been developed by many high schools and community colleges within areas where tourism revenues are significant. Mangement-oriented courses of study culminating in bachelor-level and graduate degrees are also offered at an increasing number of colleges and universities. Copies of curriculum outlines, and course descriptions are readily available. Inquiry to regional or international tourism organizations will produce lists of educational systems and institutions which can be contacted.

TRAINING

Training programs may or may not be conducted in cooperation with local school systems. Typically, large hotels, restaurant chains, and other organizations prefer to train their own personnel in accordance with their own policies and specific procedures. In most cases, large employers will arrange to set up extensive training departments. Management planners should survey these prospective employers to ascertain their needs and to offer local support as necessary; but intervention or assistance are usually unnecessary for such organizations.

There are, however, generalized skills for which publicly sponsored or supported programs can enhance job prospects. Many films and other training aids are available for persons seeking to qualify for entry-level jobs. For example, there are films and training packages on cleaning and bed making for prospective maids, there are films on techniques for waitresses, and so on. In some areas, unions or labor organizations affiliated with the government have successfully established training institutes which use this type of material or live instruction to equip individuals for entry-level opportunities.

LOCATING EDUCATIONAL AND TRAINING FACILITIES

Some physical or geographic integration between tourism facilities and institutions with associated educational or training programs is highly desirable. Because internship and apprenticeship programs are popular, proven methods for developing people in the tourism industry, schools or training facilities should be located within convenient distances of prospective places of employment. In some situations, cooperative undertakings may be possible. That is, a large hotel might actually become accredited to have its managers teach courses in which students from local schools or colleges are enrolled.

Location of educational and training facilities can become a point of concern because tourism facilities themselves are frequently located some distance from residential areas housing prospective employees. Therefore, proximity to job sites tends to be better than locations in or near residential areas.

SPECIAL HOUSING AND TRANSPORTATION REQUIREMENTS

Because tourism accommodations or attractions may be located remotely from local housing areas, special living or transportation arrangements may have to be made. These can vary widely. For example, a number of outlying resorts have dormitory-type facilities for their employees who live on premises for agreed periods, returning home for days off. In other situations, special buses or pickup services may be necessary to bring employees to facilities which are not located on public transportation routes.

As part of human-resources planning, a survey should be made and programs put into effect to provide for any special living or travel arrangements which may be necessary to support tourism-related facilities.

BUILDING A FEELING OF BELONGING

As a final point, it is worth stressing that the demands — as well as the opportunities — of a developing tourism industry will present new challenges and requirements. Most of the employees of the tourism industry are of and from the local area. Their reactions and attitudes can have a profound impact upon the long-range success and development of the tourism industry as a whole. Therefore, it becomes important that employees who are educated, developed, and sustained by the tourism industry be thought of and treated as potential goodwill ambassadors in addition to their roles as necessary resources.

SYNOPSIS

Because tourism is, overwhelmingly, a service business, a developing destination must take the steps necessary to build a pool of trained people to fill the jobs which will be created. In planning for human-resources development, programs should be established to screen and train prospective employees to satisfy two separate sets of criteria — attitudinal and technical. Attitudinal characteristics which can contribute to an employee's success in a tourism position include pride, patience, flexibility, judgment, and adaptability. Technical skills required include facilities operation, equipment operation and maintenance, financial management, food and beverage production and service, personnel management, business organization and management, and systems analysis and design. To determine needs for personnel, a staff-planning effort is recommended. This involves a series of steps which include job analysis, setting requirements and standards, preparing job descriptions, preparing job specifications, and preparing staff forecasts. This sequence of activities leads to a detailed forecast of exactly what kinds of people, with which specific qualifications and skills, will be needed at all major facilities within the tourism destination. The forecast is then analyzed to see which positions can be filled locally and which will require recruiting of specialized personnel from other areas or countries. This determination, in turn, leads to formal requests for special immigration or residence permits which may be needed by foreign employees and to development of requisite education and training programs for local residents.

REVIEW QUESTIONS

1. Explain the consequences which can result if a human-resources-development program fails to instill pride and positive attitudes in prospective tourism employees.

2. Describe the differences between service and servitude as these terms apply to positions within a tourism industry in a developing area.

3. Suppose a developing nation interested in building its tourism wishes to gain maximum employment for its own citizens and to minimize the number of foreign workers receiving special permission to reside in the country. Assume there are comparatively few local residents who have existing skills, education, or training to qualify them for tourism jobs. Under these circumstances, explain what kind of foreign specialists should be recruited and why.

4. Assuming the same situation described in Question 3, describe the major educational and training steps which should be incorporated in the human-resources plan for the area.

5. Explain why it is usually best for educational and training institutions providing tourism curricula to be located close to major tourism facilities rather than in the areas where most prospective employees reside.

17

MARKETING

THE MARKETING FUNCTION

Ultimately, a vacation involving extensive travel is a product which must be packaged and sold. Marketing is the process of identifying the product, its logical customers, and their motivations and criteria for purchasing.

Specifically, in tourism marketing, a structured program is necessary which addresses and finds answers to some specific questions, including:

- What is the product?
- Who are the potential customers?
- What do they want?
- How can they be informed that a given destination has what they want?
- How can marketing success be determined and measured?

THE PRODUCT

Tourism marketing programs sell pleasant experiences to specific groups or types of people. Tourists do not buy hotels, beaches, recreation parks, or other attractions. Thus, the important first step in planning for and executing a marketing program lies in deciding just what a destination has to sell. In doing this, there are two important, essential steps:

1. First, marketing planners should look back at the initial tourism market study which led to the development program. This should indicate the potential strengths of the destination and the markets into which they should be sold.

2. As part of the initial study also, there should have been a review of other areas which already sell the same general features or are prospective competitors. At this point, it is important to survey competitive literature and marketing programs to develop in-depth understanding of their market appeal.

By using work already done and supplementing it with some additional study, it should be possible to describe just what an area has to sell, and to whom. Emphasis within this description should be on uniqueness and particular strengths of the destination. This should be done realistically, rather than optimistically.

TARGETING SPECIFIC MARKETS

Once the product has been determined, the next step is to identify buyers. The whole premise of this book is that travel, as a product, has wide appeal. This needs no repeating here. Rather, this is the place to identify some selling specifics. Three general elements, or factors, are at work in the worldwide travel marketplace. These are:

- Geography
- Demography
- Travel professionals.

Geography

Geography is the first element considered because it tends to be the major controlling factor in tourism marketability. The term, geography, is used entirely in a travel context, stressing

217

distance between market and destination as the prime deter-
miner of the travel time and cost of vacations.

Airline representatives who had to be consulted in the course
of the market study can be of primary assistance in identifying
viable geographic markets. Representatives of international
hotel chains, if they are in the picture, can also be of help. In
addition, there are a number of directories published (one of the
most prominent is issued by the World Travel Organization)
which carry current statistics on the countries all over the world
which are primary generators of international travel activity.

Once identified, geographic market areas become the framework within which other plans can be built for tourism marketing.

Demography

Demographic factors take in specific composition of market
segments within geographic areas. These factors include age, income level, family size, nationality, fraternal-organization
membership, occupation, or other traits which establish common
denominators for marketing programs.

Demographic marketing studies should be pinpointed to individual resorts or facilities as well as to a tourism area as a
whole. For example, if a destination has a major theme park, this
would indicate a logical appeal to the family market. An area
with beaches, sports activities, and nightlife would indicate an
appeal to the so-called singles market. Culturally oriented attractions might be structured to appeal to older groups inclined
toward more leisurely travel.

The reason for demographic identification early in planning
for a marketing program is that advertising, promotional, and information media tend to be demographically oriented. This is
also true for many sales outlets.

Travel Professionals

The travel marketplace is highly structured with established
sales vehicles and outlets. Sales and media programs on behalf
of a tourism destination must be directed particularly at impress-
ing travel professionals sufficiently for them to commit the considerable selling resources they control. Without sales support
from travel professionals, success is questionable at best.

Specific travel-industry segments which must be identified for the development of any major tourism marketing program can include any or all of the following:

- Government tourism offices
- Regional travel-promotion organizations
- Airlines or other carriers
- Tour wholesalers
- Tour packagers
- Travel clubs
- Travel agents
- Convention or meeting managers.

Government Tourism Offices

These are good-will offices staffed by informed professionals who provide information on specific destinations which they represent. It behooves the sponsors to be sure that personnel in these offices have a full supply of background information and that their knowledge about the destination is updated regularly. This information should be disseminated both to other travel professionals and to prospective tourists. Thus, the location of these facilities in key prospective markets is an important part of a sales program for an area or country.

Regional Travel-Promotion Organizations

In effect, regional travel and promotion organizations perform the same functions as government tourism offices, except that they work on a collective, rather than a specialized, basis. For example, the Pacific Area Travel Association (PATA) represents all member countries and destination areas. Impartially, it distributes information and promotes interest in tourism to the Pacific. The same is true of other regional organizations, such as the European Travel Commission (ETC), and the Caribbean Travel Association (CTA).

Airlines and Other Carriers

Airlines particularly, and ship operators, railroads, and bus companies to a lesser degree, have joint stakes in building tourism business with destination areas. The airlines' situation illustrates this. A major international commercial airline has many seats to fill. A passenger seat on a specific flight is a highly perishable commodity. Once a flight departs, the inventory-value potential of the passenger seat disappears.

Airline planning and promotion are tied heavily to this fact of life. This puts airlines in a frame of mind for cooperation with managers of tourism destinations and resorts who have plans or attractions which can help them fill seats.

Thus, in planning for a marketing program, an important step should be to project potential airline passenger trips to and from the destination. Part of the marketing program will then lie in presenting these data convincingly to airline representatives. To the extent that they are in agreement about the potential of an area — and have route, schedule, and fare authorization, as well as flexibility — they are in a position to alter routes, schedules, or fares to help promote travel to a given destination. Airlines are also in a position to muster awesome marketing support for an individual area through international advertising and specific sales activities on the part of their own ticket agents and travel agents who cooperate. In addition, airlines also function as major wholesalers and packagers of tours.

Tour Wholesalers

Tour wholesalers, as the name implies, are in the business of buying accommodations and reservations in volume, at a discount, and selling them at a profit. A wholesaler begins by planning a vacation program for a known market segment — usually in seven, 10, or 14-day, all-inclusive increments. The wholesaler books the necessary hotel and travel reservations to accommodate a projected number of customers and to maximize discount leverage. Where popular attractions or restaurants add to the appeal of a package, advance reservations can also be made for these.

The wholesaler then puts together all of the brochures and other media necessary to offer the tours through established travel-market outlets. As reservations are booked, tourists are asked to pay deposits on their trips. At this point, the wholesaler firms up reservations for hotels and travel seats and makes arrangements for ground transportation, meals, and other accommodations which require less lead time. As with any other product which is marketed, the wholesaler realizes a profit by charging more than the accommodations and reservations cost, including allowances for promotion and cost of sales.

Tour Packagers

A tour packager is much like a wholesaler except that no financial commitments are made by these entrepreneurs. Rather, tour packagers subsist by selling their services to wholesalers or others. In effect, they sell their knowledge of destinations and travel markets. They secure commitments from hotels, airlines, and others, putting together all of the elements of a tour. After that, wholesalers, airlines, or others take over, respecting the commitments and carrying through with marketing.

Travel Clubs

The role and operation of travel clubs were discussed in the chapter on transportation. Within the context of this discussion, it is relevant to recognize that travel clubs are managed by professionals who should figure in the marketing program for a major tourism destination. Travel clubs may be managed by airline representatives, tour packagers, travel agents, or full-time employees of sponsoring organizations. Wherever they are situated, these travel professionals should be included in the communication and sales plans for a tourism destination which can profit from the volumes of business they represent.

Travel Agents

Travel agents are the retailers of the tourism industry. They set up outlets in retail centers, frequently in stores. They sell tickets, reservations, and spaces in group tours. Where tickets are sold, the travel agent keeps a commission, remitting the difference to the carrier or tour operator. Where reservations are made, as in the case of hotels, the facility operator remits a commission to the agent. The travel industry has built up a series of organizations which oversee and handle these exchanges of payments between travel facilities, carriers, and retail agents.

A travel agency is a special kind of retailer in that it is impossible to bring the product to customers. The main thing a travel agent is selling, then, is research and knowledge about travel and vacation opportunities which will be of interest to specific customers. The travel agent collects information about destination areas and resorts, collects information on fare and price structures, and frequently becomes personally familiar with prime vacation areas of interest to a specific clientele. The overall idea is to acquire and sell knowledgeability.

In planning to market an area or resort within a given geographic and demographic structure, it becomes essential to deliver information to and to educate travel agents who reach these identified consumers. The initial objective is to build enthusiasm among travel agents to sell a specific area. To maintain this enthusiasm, and level of activity, it then becomes vital that arrangements be made to honor financial commitments to travel agents. Delays in paying commissions or haggling over amounts can quickly diminish market potential, since travel agents belong to organizations which distribute this kind of information rapidly and thoroughly.

Convention or Meeting Managers

Part of the planning for a tourism industry lies in determining whether there is a potential to attract conventions or major meetings. If so, it becomes important to: 1) provide suitable facilities, and 2) identify and reach managers who make arrangements for meetings and conventions which can be accommodated.

A major characteristic of large meetings or conventions is that they are scheduled far in advance — frequently five to seven years, depending upon their size. Generally, the larger the convention, the longer the range of its planning. A number of directories are published which identify regularly held meetings by type, size, facilities required, and season or month in which they are usually held. If an area wants this type of business, it becomes necessary to develop a program for contacting interested managers. Frequently, it is necessary to offer these key people cost-free vacations as part of the selling effort.

IDENTIFYING CHANNELS OF COMMUNICATION

One of the big challenges, particularly in building an identification for a tourism area strange to residents of its major market, lies in combatting and overcoming a natural fear of the unknown. By definition, new tourists are strangers. Strangeness, in turn, can breed apprehension. Many tourists tend to have concerns about food, infection, disease, discomfort, inconvenience, language barriers, and simply putting themselves at the mercy of strangers. Advertising and promotion campaigns frequently must overcome these natural concerns and fears before people start visiting an area. This, incidentally, is one reason why packaged tours tend to be so popular in the introductory phase of the building of a new tourism attraction or area: the very existence of a group of people collectively willing to face something unknown tends to encourage all of the participants.

Advertising and promotional programs require specifically qualified, experienced managers. Arrangements should be made to secure services of people who are familiar with the media in the major markets as well as with the travel industry. This can be done by engaging an advertising agency, by hiring a qualified specialist, or a combination of both. Media, outlets, or programs in which a tourism destination may find itself involved include:

- Informative literature
- Direct mail
- Space advertising (print media)
- Broadcast time advertising
- Public relations and publicity
- Advertising signs.

Informative Literature

The stock in trade for a tourism communication program is a series of brochures, information sheets, letters, bulletins, and other printed media which can be sent to both marketing outlets and prospective tourists. These items are also referred to as promotional literature. However, the term, informative literature, was chosen because this is where the emphasis belongs. Consider: the purpose of the entire program is to build confidence which will pave the way for sales. The best way to do this is with reliable information, believably presented.

"Slick" brochures are not always best. For some market segments, for example, it is far more desirable to show realistic photographs than idealized drawings. Content should be factual; glowing, exaggerated descriptions may be more harmful than convincing.

Prospective tourists and the travel professionals who sell to them really want facts. They want to know about climate, the prospects of rain, temperature, quality of accommodations, types of food available, and any special precautions they should take, such as immunization, etc. Information included in informative literature should be both practical and helpful. For example, it will be appreciated if prospective tourists are advised to bring plenty of suntan lotion. This type of advice is accepted as a practical hint. The effect of such advice is to convince the reader that the destination does, in fact, have potent sunshine. In general, also, it is better to feature one or two strong points than to try to depict a full story about an area and its features in a one or two-page document.

Direct Mail

Direct-mail advertising can be a primary marketing technique for a tourism area or facility because of the potential afforded for identifying and pinpointing specific audiences.

In general, two separate market segments are susceptible to the direct-mail approach:

- Travel professionals
- Persons who travel frequently.

With both segments of the market, the key to success lies in securing and maintaining effective lists of names and addresses. To implement programs, it is possible to buy extensively coded geographic and demographic lists from experienced suppliers. These organizations can provide services ranging from just mailing labels through to complete printing, envelope stuffing, and mailing services.

Tracking returns from direct-mail campaigns can be one of the fastest, most flexible means of identifying the real market potential for any tourism area. Direct mail is valuable in this respect because programs can be implemented at the convenience of the advertiser. It is not necessary to wait for publication schedules, or to go through extensive production required by television or radio commercials. Existing literature with simplified covering letters can usually be used. Lists can be generated by computers almost overnight. Responses begin to arrive and can be evaluated in a matter of weeks.

Lists of travel professionals usually derive from memberships of organizations to which they belong. Lists of affluent individual travelers are derived, most typically, from credit-card plans, professional directories of persons in affluent occupations, or airline or other charge accounts. Some computer-maintained lists are compiled through occupational cross referencing of charge-account data. It has become possible, recently, for example, to develop lists of doctors, attorneys, accountants, or other professionals who have actually run up fairly large international-exchange charges with leading credit-card plans.

One effective approach is to go to vendors of direct-mail services with the profile of a tourism destination's target audience. Two or more vendors can be invited to present proposals. In this field, it can be advantageous to create competitive situations.

Space Advertising

Space advertising gets its name from the fact that the advertiser contracts to use space in a publication — newspaper, magazine, directory, or other medium. The advertiser or agency develops the message to be carried in the contracted space. Advertising-space programs are generally incorporated within campaigns which include extensive plans to reach given geographic and demographic audiences.

Within the tourism or travel industries, advertising in these "print" media reaches two general types of audiences — travel professionals and consumers. Promotional programs typically balance exposure between consumers and travel professionals. The principal is that consumers who see an ad about a destination area or resort in a magazine are sold on the image or idea of a future visit. This leads them to talk to an airline representative or travel agent, who, in turn, has also been introduced to the area or resort through advertising in specialized industry magazines.

Broadcast Time Advertising

Broadcast time includes commercial spots or program sponsorship on radio or television. This is almost entirely a consumer medium. Broadcast media are, typically, used on a seasonal or impulse basis. For example, if an area has a prime tourism season, heavy use of broadcast media prior to the time when tourist visits are expected should stimulate business.

Public Relations and Publicity

Publicity is the specific act of offering information or articles to broadcast or print media for their editorial use. With reputable publications or outlets, there should be no charge to the sponsoring organization for use of these materials. The only cost lies in writing, production, and distribution. It does, however, take a knowledgeable person to understand the market, to know what types of materials editors use, and to cultivate the personal contacts which encourage editors to use some stories in preference to others.

Public relations is more encompassing. It includes the planning and staging of events which are candidates for publicity or advertising promotion. Typical public relations activities include the planning of celebrity visits, the scheduling of sponsored, expense-paid "familiarization" trips to the area by travel agents or media editors, the offering of sites for motion picture production, and so on.

Public relations and publicity programs are carried out both on a staff and on an agency basis.

Advertising Signs

Because travel sales are largely on impulse, many travel organizations, destination areas, and resorts have found it effective to use billboards and other advertising signs in their promotional campaigns.

This segment of the advertising industry has established standards to which advertisers conform. One, for example, is the so-called 24-sheet billboard. This derives its name from a standard size and from the practice of printing signs to be affixed to the billboards in 24 separate sheets identified by grid location. The same type of standard also applies to smaller signs typically used in airports, railroad stations, or bus stations.

All of these media and potential information outlets play integrated roles within a marketing campaign which provides the real challenge for bringing profitable levels of tourism traffic into an area or to a resort.

DEVELOPING A MARKETING CAMPAIGN

A marketing program for a developing tourism area falls, logically and necessarily, into two separate, distinct phases: startup and ongoing operation. Both are necessary and important.

If a destination area is new in the tourism market or has been substantially expanded, startup planning is particularly critical.

This is because a disproportionately large percentage of problems and failures are experienced in serving the first guests into a new area. There is a potential impact on the total success or failure of the area, since word-of-mouth is the strongest and most convincing sales support a tourism destination or resort can have. Thus, if things are fouled up at the beginning, there is danger of a built-in, long-range negative impact. Conversely, a good experience at the beginning greatly enhances prospects of success.

For this reason, extreme care should be exercised in the setting of an official opening date for a new destination or resort. A good practice is to take a logical opening date, the day on which all parties are sure everything can be brought together and be ready for operation, then extend it for about a month or six weeks, using this later date as the official opening.

There is a temptation, as a resort or area comes close to the final stages of an extended, expensive development program, to permit anxiety for cash flow to overcome prudence. The tendency is to set the scheduled opening date as early as possible. This should be resisted.

If, in fact, a facility or area is ready for business prior to a conservatively set opening date, this time can usually be sold simply by plugging it into the promotional and marketing mechanisms which have been established by then. As another alternative, limited numbers of discounted packages can be sold to bring guests into the area to give personnel a chance to "shake down" the operation before guests identified as primary marketing targets begin to arrive.

Part of the special consideration associated with startup budgets is that these expenses should and can be regarded as part of the capital costs of going into business. Careful consideration should be given to the prospects for capitalizing such expenses as recoverable through operating profits at a later date. Such practices can have a favorable impact on ownership balances and taxation.

Further, the amount of money allocated to startup programs can have an impact upon the budgets for ongoing promotion. In effect, the budget for ongoing promotion maintains the image and position established by the startup program. Thus, the ongoing program budget should relate to and provide logical continuity for the startup allocation.

Planning Media and Sales Campaigns

In both the startup and ongoing program areas, separate attention should be paid to media campaigns and actual selling programs. Both should be related, since the media programs condition the market for the actual selling effort. It is pointless to hire salesmen, give them briefcases full of literature, and send them out to call on prospective customers who may never have heard of an area or resort. Thus, the heaviest use of media should usually be at the "front end" of a marketing program. This should be tailored to reach the people who will be approached by the selling organization.

In the tourism industry, the selling organization spends most of its time dealing with travel professionals. Members of the sales staff are generally situated in or near the major markets identified as prime targets. Sales territories are set up in much the same manner as the planning of sales coverage for a manufactured product. These staff persons would establish information offices to which prospective tourists are invited. In addition, members of the staff would expedite visas or tourist cards for prospective visitors and would attend meetings and call upon travel wholesalers, packagers, airline representatives, and travel agents.

All of the activities of media and selling programs should, of course, be coordinated on an overall basis by the management of the destination or resort. A plan should be set up so that information about tourists can be correlated with expenditures and efforts of the marketing program itself.

EVALUATION

It is important to establish methods which measure the effectiveness of sales and promotional programs continuously. To the greatest extent possible, data collection and analysis programs should identify amounts and sources of revenue realized. These data should be accumulated and reported in terms of targeted geographic and demographic audiences. Revenues should be related to advertising and sales-promotion budgets. These data should then become a basis for allocating or redirecting funds for ongoing promotional budgets.

Actually, the data collected and analyzed will depend upon the ability of any given area or resort to collect them. For example, if most of a destination's visitors arrive from other countries, it is relatively simple to incorporate questionnaires into entry/departure (E/D) forms which are part of visa or travel-card documents. Substantial geographic and demographic data can be accumulated in this way. In addition, departure data gathering can include questions on length of stay and amount of money spent, as well as satisfaction with the host area.

Where arrival in an area is primarily by auto or surface transportation, collection of useful data can be more difficult. Whatever the situation of the individual area or resort, however, plans should be made to collect the most data feasible, to analyze them, and to apply derived information in future promotion and sales budgets and programs.

SYNOPSIS

Tourists "buy" a pleasant experience. Their concern is for enjoyment rather than for individual facilities or arrangements. Most tourists are happy to leave details associated with planning their journeys to travel professionals. Contacts with and support of travel professionals are among the key factors for successful marketing of a tourism destination. (Others are geography — distance between a tourism destination and its prospective markets — and demography — the tastes, age, financial position, and family status of prospective tourists.) Facilities and specialties of travel professionals include government tourism offices, regional travel-promotion organizations, airlines or other carriers, tour wholesalers, tour packagers, travel clubs, travel agents, and convention or meeting managers. Channels of communication used to inform and stimulate the tourism marketplace include informative literature, direct mail, space advertising, broadcast time advertising, public relations and publicity, and advertising signs. These media are selected and organized into campaigns aimed at selling both consumers and travel professionals. The media campaigns are timed to correspond with the selling effort supporting a destination or resort. Data gathering should be built into operations of tourism facilities to make possible comparisons between sales results and promotional expenditures.

REVIEW QUESTIONS

1. It is said that tourists buy pleasant experiences rather than concentrating on specific facilities and arrangements. Discuss this characteristic of tourism marketing and its implications for programs aimed at drawing visitors into an area.

2. Describe the role of travel professionals associated with government or area-promotion agencies in the promotion of tourism.

3. Describe the functions of tour packagers and wholesalers in building tourism markets.

4. Discuss the principles of and needs for coordination between media promotion and sales programs in tourism marketing.

18

EVALUATION AND DIRECTION FOR CONTINUING GROWTH

POST-IMPLEMENTATION REVIEW

Planning and implementing a tourism-development program constitutes a major project. As a project, this effort will have a predefined termination point — a time when the developmental effort ends. If all goes well, this will be a point of transition from development into a profitable, ongoing tourism industry and/or entity. For this to happen, additional, special planning and implementation efforts are· required. One of these is a post-implementation review.

After the project phase of a tourism-development program is complete, there should be a planned, coordinated program of data gathering, reporting, evaluation, and decision making aimed at determining how successful the program has·been and how successes can be used as building blocks and failures or weaknesses overcome. This process is, in effect, a reporting and surveying exercise like the one which preceded entry into the tourism-development endeavor. Its purpose is to report on achievement as compared with objectives and to produce recommendations on where the tourism industry should go in the immediate, intermediate, and long-range future.

As indicated earlier, it is a sound practice to start a tourism-development program with a five-year *pro forma* operating plan. This should be reviewed and updated cyclically, each six or 12 months. After the tourism project has been implemented, this plan becomes the basis for management of ongoing operations.

MONITORING ONGOING OPERATIONS

Data should be collected, interpreted, and reported on a regular, cycled basis to indicate the status of tourism operations. Depending on the entity involved, it may be desirable to have daily, weekly, monthly, seasonal, or quarterly reports. The frequency and detailing of these reports will depend upon the position and responsibility of recipients. For example, government-agency managers involved in marketing, monitoring, or regulating tourism facilities might find they can operate satisfactorily with monthly reports. By contrast, the manager of an individual, major hotel, may need daily occupancy data.

Sources of this operating and status data have been described previously. Within an ongoing industry, the objective is to analyze and use pertinent information as a management tool. Thus, reports would be formatted to show comparative figures on seasonal occupancy, geographic and demographic analysis of income, and so on.

Also important within an ongoing industry or entity is a monitoring of quality. One typical way that this function is performed is for a government-operated service to inspect hotels and other facilities and to rate their actual performance in comparison with standards which were established previously. It is important that these reports be produced regularly, made known to management of the facilities, and acted upon where a deterioration in service or quality has set in.

In summary, there is a time when tourism development stops being a project and goes through the transition into an ongoing business. Managers must make the transition within the reality of their own situations. Certainly there is no shortage of advice or literature about management techniques. This book will not attempt to cross the bridge into how to manage operational businesses. Rather, in addressing the topic of tourism planning and development, it is critical to recognize that there is a point when development ends and maintenance begins. At this point, the consultants and project people either leave or make a transition into employee status. Techniques for management continuity take over.

INDEX

INDEX